A JOHN CATT PUBLICATION

CURRICULUM
REVOLUTIONS

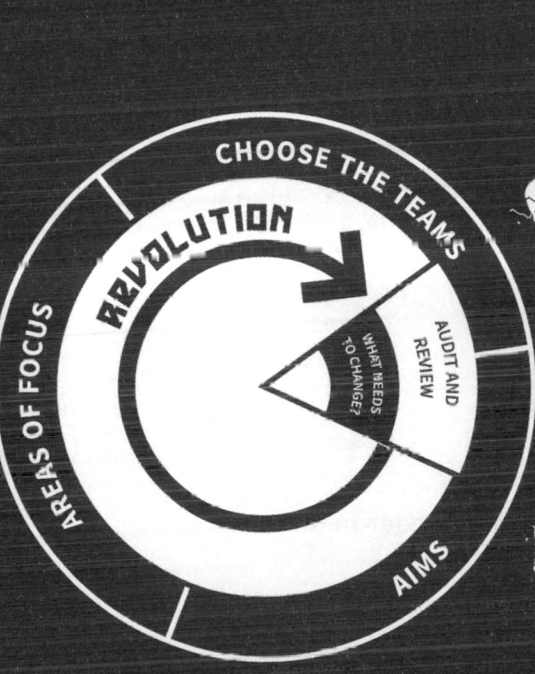

**Cover design and illustrations
by David Goodwin**

A PRACTICAL GUIDE TO
ENHANCING WHAT YOU TEACH

MARTIN ROBINSON

First published 2022

by John Catt Educational Ltd,
15 Riduna Park, Station Road,
Melton, Woodbridge IP12 1QT

Tel: +44 (0) 1394 389850
Email: enquiries@johncatt.com
Website: www.johncatt.com

ISBN: 978 1 913622 98 5

Set and designed by John Catt Educational Limited

Foreword

When ideas appear to be in opposition, there is often a temptation, even a kind of pressure, to pick sides. Which side are you on? Alternatively, there is a tendency to fudge the issue; to soften the boundaries and carve out some middle ground; to find a third way, as if opposing ideas can be resolved. However, as Martin Robinson has demonstrated time and again, sometimes the wisest thing to do is just to embrace the conflict; to engage in the debate and make progress through holding ideas in constant tension. This is the essence of the journey captured in Martin's first magnificent book, *Trivium 21c*. Here, he argues that it is only through providing space for the grammar (knowing, tradition) and the dialectic (questioning, debating, exploring) of the trivium, not favouring one over the other, that we arrive at a curriculum that meets the needs of modern society.

Martin writes:

Schools should develop a curriculum that responds to change as well as being rooted in a sensitive awareness of our traditions and how they are evolving. It should seek out academic, cultural, social, artistic, and physical challenges that are authentic, that stretch each child and give them experiences they would not otherwise get.

... In a true democracy all citizens share responsibility for their community. We need to educate all young people to be philosopher kids, to be part of the philosopher crowds, finding their way through the global village.[1]

---

[1]   Robinson, M. (2013) *Trivium 21c: preparing young people for the future with lessons from the past*, Independent Thinking Press

Over the near decade since *Trivium 21c* was published, schools have continued to wrestle with the thorny issues of developing and implementing the curriculum they believe their children deserve. And it's complicated! There's so much to learn and only so much time to teach it in. Every curriculum plan is a record of decisions made – what to teach and when – but also, by default, it represents a kind of negative of everything that's been left out. As teachers and school leaders soon realise, these decisions are never-ending. The job is never done. And here lies the challenge: balancing time to design a curriculum alongside teaching it is like attempting to re-engineer a fast car while driving it at full speed. Very obviously, this can't be done. At least, it can't be done well by each individual teacher working alone, with all the expertise required.

This is where Martin's new book, *Curriculum Revolutions*, comes to our aid. Once again, he deftly explores the tensions in the concepts to find the answers. A curriculum revolution is not necessarily a fundamental or sudden change; the curriculum design process goes round and round! A continually revolving process lies at the heart of this excellent guide to curriculum design.

Alongside the tensions within the content of the curriculum, Martin introduces and explores the tensions in principle and practice around who decides that content. Teacher autonomy can be important: that freedom to navigate a curriculum domain with your students, with elements of spontaneity and quirky off-piste trips into the hinterland, is highly prized. But, surely, we need a curriculum to have coherence for students far beyond the role each teacher plays – it's not all about us! Our work forms part of something much bigger, deeper and wider; something that needs to make sense to a student overall and over the long run.

In addition, there's the workload issue. Why continually reinvent our individualistic wheels if, through collaboration in teams, we can devise a more coherent curriculum with resources we can all use, saving precious time and energy in the process?

In this book, Martin sets out an excellent set of practical curriculum design tools linked through the visual metaphor of interlocking wheels. Each wheel goes round again and again at the rate necessary for the task in hand. Teachers can use the ideas here to scope out a long-term design process and to consider whether curriculum decisions are best made by individual teachers or by the team.

As well as putting these wheels in motion, Martin introduces a superb set of organising schema in the form of curriculum trees. Each tree offers a different way of thinking about curriculum content, so that what students learn adds up to something much greater than a never-ending procession through one thing after another.

So if, from the title of this book, you're expecting some kind of revolutionary anarchy, well, you won't find it here. That would be misplaced, because there is serious business at hand – our trivium-inspired philosopher kids won't emerge from chaos. Instead, you'll find a powerful conceptual framework, designed with the artful craftsmanship of a beautiful clock and insightful understanding of how teachers thrive – neither always alone nor always in collaboration, but forever part of a continuing bold and ambitious process best achieved together.

Tom Sherrington
Author of *The Learning Rainforest* and *Teaching WalkThrus*

Contents

Introduction

Gone are the days when a teacher could turn up on a Monday morning, check the newspaper, choose a couple of articles and photocopy them ready for each child to 'do some work on'. Gone are the days of the drunken chat with a colleague in a pub that became a whole new scheme of work photocopied and ready for pupils the next day. Also gone are the days of the head of department suggesting to the newly minted teacher, as happened to me when I began to teach English in a secondary school, 'See what's in the stock cupboard or take a look in the filing cabinet. You're sure to find something to suit you there and, if you want, adapt it or, hey, do your own thing!'

This was how things were when I got into teaching and, well, I loved it. I loved the freedom. I was an artist – I made wonderful things happen, my pupils learned wonderful things. This anarchy was extremely creative, but I had little understanding of what went before or what was to follow. Each teacher was an island. The knowledge they had to impart was individualised, usually by each teacher's own knowledge and/or enthusiasms. It was sometimes eccentric and often inspiring, but not part of an unfolding narrative that required me to teach content that built on what went before, helping the child to grow academically as they went from class to class and year to year.

We might get away with this anarchic approach if our pupils are culturally mobile and understand a lot. Our lessons are merely the 'icing on the cake' of their already broad expanse of knowledge. But most pupils are not this fortunate. In fact, very, very few would have the prerequisite amount of knowledge across the wide range of subjects they are exposed to in the average school to enable them to cope with all the subjects with the competence of an advanced scholar. They might be able to kick a ball successfully into a goal and to read a book pitched at their age group, or any number of other abilities, but the breadth of knowledge required at school is that of a budding polymath.

Now imagine the opposite to this anarchic approach. The most mechanical and dehumanising approach, where the teacher is akin to a call centre operative, deskilled on the day they are given their script by the director of the department of dehumanisation or the CEO of geography, or whatever their title is. Here's your script, your resources – DO NOT DEVIATE, says the dalek. Some argue that an actor still has creative freedom aplenty when they deliver their lines, and this is true, but they tend to have a rather richer script – an actual 'character' enabling them to focus on the richness of the human condition rather than how to conjugate a verb.

Between the joyful anarchy of last-minute planning and the authoritarian delivery of the curriculum by numbers, there must be a place that can capture the freedom of thought of the former and the need for consistency addressed by the latter. This book hopes to find that happy spot.

Thoughtful curriculum design

The importance of a thoughtful approach to curriculum design cannot be underestimated. Pupils can flourish in their learning if a curriculum is cohesive, coherent and periodically reviewed in the context of changing knowledge and culture, as well as governmental, international and local needs and desires. *Curriculum Revolutions* is built around a process – a tool – that can help you to approach curriculum design through a continuous cycle of planning, designing, delivering, reflecting and reviewing. This process will involve your managers, teachers and pupils in ensuring all understand the importance of a well-functioning curriculum as the cornerstone of the school and the education it delivers.

Good curriculum design is a collaborative affair. Teachers must be given time to work together to create curricula in which they all have a say (the collegiate nature of schools is one of the reasons so many of us love – or loved – teaching).

The creativity of the teaching staff, absorbed in creating a joined-up curriculum for their pupils, ensures that the curriculum has buy-in from the teachers, as they can take responsibility for its successes and any problems that might be found en route. Every teacher understands their role in delivering a cohesive curriculum; they understand what has been taught before and what will be taught next by themselves and their colleagues. Even if the maverick teacher closes the classroom door and goes 'off-piste', they are more aware of how and where they fit into the whole, and how essential it is that they pass the baton on in the curriculum relay, allowing other teachers – and their pupils – to run with it.

In this relay, each teacher should be aware of what they are doing, what went before and what happens afterwards. To mix our metaphors, each teacher presents but a chapter of a novel and, in order to do this successfully, they must know the overall narrative in detail.

How to start a revolution

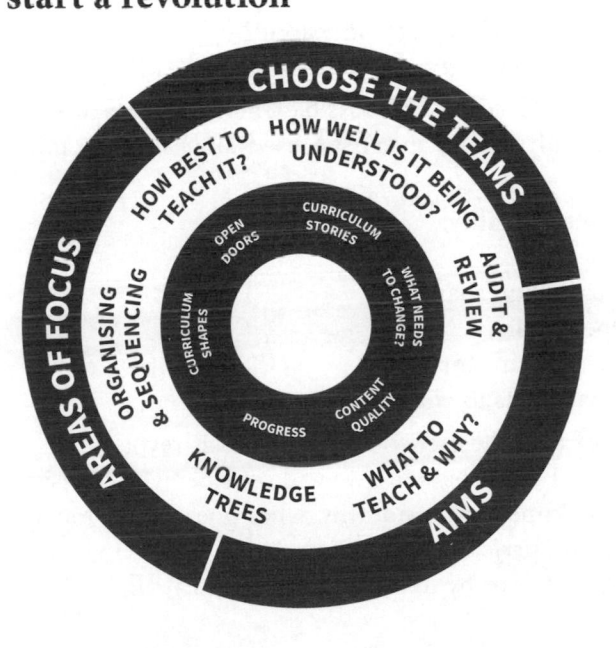

A curriculum revolution takes us around one or more of the concentric circles you see in the wheel on the previous page. There is the outer circle, a preliminary revolution that sets up the process; a middle circle that functions as the main vehicle for focusing on curriculum design; and an inner circle that adds a layer of more detailed thinking to your curriculum design approach.

Let's look at the 'stops' on our curriculum revolution. The **outer circle** provides a focus for management from a whole institutional perspective. It has three stops:

1. Aims.
2. Areas of focus.
3. Choose the teams.

The other two revolutions are for the curriculum teams themselves and form the basis of most of this book. The **middle circle** is the main 'ipsative' process, or 'permanent revolution':

1. What to teach and why?
2. Knowledge trees.
3. Organising and sequencing.
4. How best to teach it?
5. How well is it being understood?
6. Audit and review.

The **inner circle** considers possible improvements where a bit more nuance is required, and it can be used alongside the middle circle or instead of it:

1. Content quality.
2. Progress.
3. Curriculum shapes.
4. Open doors.
5. Curriculum stories.
6. What needs to change?

Each part of the wheel encountered in each revolution is discussed in chapters 2-10. But in chapter 1 we will consider why cohesive curriculum design is so important, and why what goes on in too many schools disrupts good curriculum thinking, either by leaving too much to the individual teacher or by not trusting teachers at all.

1. Achieving curriculum cohesion

In many schools around the world, teachers are, rightly, treated as most trusted professionals. When they close the classroom door, they can forget all the outside pressures that management place upon them – data-chasing, performance targets and so on. Instead, they can do what many, if not most, teachers like best: teach. Pupils are often inspired and may even have their lives changed by their engagement with their teacher.

This process has many strengths. It also has at least one major flaw: pupils are not usually taught by the same teacher for their entire time at school. If they were to be taught by one teacher then their experience would be, in most cases, pretty consistent – the teacher would naturally gravitate towards some sort of consistency in curriculum approach. They would refer to lessons they had taught before and point to where a nugget of knowledge might lead to in the future. They would, if a good teacher, accept responsibility for when things weren't well understood, reconstruct when things went awry and resolve any misconceptions. This consistency in approach is, of course, infinitely adaptable.

The problem arises when many teachers are encountered over a pupil's time at school. One teacher might describe how to write a sentence in one way, another teacher in another way. One teacher might describe an atom in one way, another teacher in another way. The first explanation of an atom might be simple, because that might be all that is necessary at the time, but later, in another class, it might be important to add some detail. Similarly, experienced readers may 'sense' and absorb the qualities of a sentence, but other pupils who don't read much might struggle without clear, concise and cohesive explanations. The braver ones might ask and the teacher might give a quick explanation, but another teacher might explain it differently or the explanations might even contradict each other. Further explanations require the teacher to know what the original explanations were, and for the original teacher to explain that further explanations will come in due course.

Sometimes, the 'curriculum' is a by-product of teachers making do with resources and materials and 'schemes of work' that have accumulated over the years. In order to alleviate this problem, a few schools have written scripts for teachers to follow. This highly centralised, 'authoritarian' approach can result in a cohesive curriculum, but often lacks buy-in from teachers who might not agree with the script, or with some of the choices made around content and its sequencing.

Many schools use textbooks, although these can be of varying quality. Some teachers use textbooks religiously, others dip in and out, and still others prefer to teach 'their way'. Some subjects lend themselves to textbook teaching more than others: maths and science teachers might look aghast at arts and humanities teachers as they rail against textbooks or appear to make things up as they go along…OK, I'm stereotyping here, just to make a point. But differing buy-ins from individual teachers lead to inconsistencies that may need to be ironed out if huge (or even moderately sized) gaps in knowledge are uncovered among pupils as they reach the end of their courses. The discovery of such gaps can lead to panic-teaching, which rarely results in pupils knowing more, focusing as it does on ways to get through end-of-course assessments and exams, rather than on building knowledge that could help young people to lead more fulfilling lives. Cramming classes after school and during holidays are desperate remedies for a curriculum that has failed and should not be seen as a successful 'support' for pupils; rather, they create stress and can lead to unhealthy levels of unnecessary anxiety.

National and local curricula may be introduced but these can be used very differently by individual teachers, unless compliance is strictly mandated. 'Are they obeying the authorities?' becomes the mantra as inspectors are tasked with finding out what goes on behind classroom doors.

There is, however, another way: *collaborative design*. In this approach, the collective thoughts of teachers dictate the curriculum. Teachers must resolve their differences, coming to an excellent understanding of the curriculum because they can see the detailed content they are teaching day-to-day, as well as the 'grand scheme of things' and how they fit into it. Collaborative curriculum design takes more time, at least at first. But in the long term it is healthier for collegiate support and professional development, better for schools and, most importantly, better for pupils. Rather than being, potentially, befuddled and stressed, pupils can begin to see how knowledge connects and makes sense, and where knowledge might be uncertain and/or create discussion and argument. A good curriculum helps pupils to make meaning of the world and to find their place within the great debates and ideas, knowing and thinking for themselves.

Thinking for yourself is an interesting concept. Where does a thought come from? Thinking is not an individual process, because none of us is an island thinking entirely for ourselves; we do not exist separately to the world. Our social and cultural being shapes our thoughts, as do our feelings and physical perspectives. If we therefore take it for granted that the world around a child helps to shape how the child thinks and makes meaning, then we can see how a good curriculum is important. A good curriculum helps a child to think about and understand the world, to make sense of who they are and to cope with the changing understanding they might have in the future.

This brings us to an important realisation. How well a pupil is learning is not entirely about them – *it is about all of us*. And yet we often use assessment just to measure how well they are doing, rather than to think about how well *we* are doing. A successful curriculum is one that can be seen to make a difference. One way to ensure it is successful is for teachers to take responsibility for the quality of learning of their pupils.

The cohesion continuum

Once we begin to consider that how a pupil is doing in their studies might be less to do with their individual performance, less to do with the teacher and more to do with the curriculum, the better we can understand the curriculum's importance. A good number of our pupils, for example, might struggle to write a coherent essay. Instead of thinking of this as a problem with 'our kids' or 'our staff', start to think of it as a problem with 'our curriculum'. Consider how much teaching time, over a period of lessons, is devoted to the explicit teaching of how to write an essay. When pupils are struggling with any topic, the first port of call should be: where does this feature in our curriculum, explicitly?

It is so important that teachers are part of permanent curriculum revolutions. Not in the way of one teacher taking responsibility for designing a part of the curriculum and expecting others to follow, but in a process of co-creation, so that everyone has a deep understanding of the underlying structure and logic of what is being taught and how it unfolds over time. In some schools this will require headteachers themselves to be more involved and knowledgeable about curriculum design; in others it will require principals and managers to cede more decision-making responsibility to their middle managers. Mostly, it should involve giving more power over to teachers. This revolution is not just about circular planning processes, but also about flatter management structures. The heart of collaborative curriculum planning is trusting in teachers and helping them to design, review and critically engage with curriculum conversations and decision-making.

It is the job of the headteacher/principal/leadership team to launch discussions about curriculum cohesion. In order to check how close your school is to a cohesive approach to curriculum, the first question to ask is: where is our school and each curriculum area on the *cohesion continuum*?

Where are you on the continuum?

1   2   3   4   5   6   7   8   9   10

Teacher autonomy   **Scripted lessons**

The aim here is to see the problems with the hyper-authoritarian approach at one end of the continuum, and with the looser anarchic approach at the other end.

Each teacher can be asked to give their department and/or school a score of 1-10 on the curriculum cohesion continuum. They write down the number and share it with their colleagues. This can lead to discussions about strengths and weaknesses, the differences between staff members' perspectives, and what might change for better or worse with more cohesion. All this can be done anonymously at first – a very good step, especially in a low-trust environment where it can begin to open up a more honest dialogue between teachers and leaders.

The outcome of the discussions tends to leave a problem: how can we collaborate to reach cohesiveness, rather than leave too much to individual teachers? How can we avoid teachers taking part in an anarchic free-for-all or becoming robotic delivery machines? This is where the cohesion questionnaire comes in.

The curriculum cohesion questionnaire

Once the school's cohesiveness has been explored through more informal discussion, it is time to investigate the issues in a bit more depth. The curriculum cohesion questionnaire can aid this process, helping to identify how much of a school's curriculum is down to individual teachers making decisions about what to teach and, indeed, how to teach it.

First, go over the two extremes on the curriculum cohesion continuum, from the most anarchic teacher who is totally free to do whatever they want, to the teacher who has no choice over what, when and how they teach. Next, use the questionnaire to consider where teachers believe the school and its curriculum areas are on the cohesion continuum.

1. **How much autonomy is currently granted to teachers individually to teach in their own way? Why and to what effect?**

   Discuss this in relation to different parts of the curriculum, including co-curricular/extracurricular provision, subjects where teachers are not necessarily experts, and even cover lessons. What are the teachers expected to do? These minimum expectations need to be made clear at the outset. If better solutions are found then, of course, the minimum expectations could be adaptable but, in the main, they remain non-negotiables.

2. **Do we know what our colleagues are teaching, why and when, in our own subject as well as other relevant subjects?**

   To find this out, teachers can be asked to write their answers down at the same time, or they can be interviewed about the curriculum in real depth, separately. It might be interesting to compare their answers with the school's planned curriculum. Ask teachers, individually, what they know about what they teach, what comes before, where it leads to and how this connects to other subject areas.

3. **What are our priorities for the development of the curriculum and why?**

   Once the degree of curriculum connectivity has been established, it is a good time to look at where you are and where you want to be in establishing a cohesive curriculum design. Departmental/area curriculum planning needs to reflect where things are, where they ought to be and how to get there.

4. **How much time do teachers in each area spend collaborating on curriculum design each year? What is the evidence for this?**

   Asking teachers this question individually might elicit a range of answers. It is important that schools make time for formal curriculum collaboration as well as enabling opportunities for informal discussion. I call this 'open doors'; other terms include 'water-cooler moments'.

5. **Do teachers have a clear idea of how the overall curriculum progresses throughout the school?**

   Of course, it is most important that teachers understand progression in their own subjects, but an overview of other areas/subjects might be useful, especially when it comes to cross-curricular themes, skills and knowledge – e.g. statistics, graphs, essay-writing, reading, and historical and cultural literacy.

   Progress in subjects is very much about how the curriculum terrain is mapped out. Subjects like maths could be mapped out on a ladder, while others, like English, seem to be more amorphous, lacking an obvious hierarchy but arguably covering more ground in a shallower way. The strictly hierarchal nature of maths means that pupils must learn the basics of number and place value before they have the requisite knowledge to progress on to algebra. At the other end of the scale, the shallower hierarchies in English mean that sequencing the subject is much less obvious. Most subjects fall somewhere between these extremes.

Understanding how we map our subject's terrain is crucial as decisions about progress must be inherently empirical (based on how children actually learn the thing) and inherently local (what we choose to focus on is our choice.) So, in maths, although progression through solving equations must begin with number and place value, there are different possible pathways to take once the basics are mastered. In English, on the other hand, once pupils have learned the foundational knowledge of phonics and letter formation, there are an almost infinite number of directions that a curriculum could take.

6. How could we improve how we collect evidence about the curriculum, in terms of how it is planned, taught and its effect on pupils? Do we consider the evidence to be relevant and adequate?

7. How could the results of this evaluation help to set the priorities for the next steps needed in curriculum design?

   The findings from the questions above should be reported to all staff. The next four questions can be used to draw conclusions from the evidence gathered.

8. How joined-up is teachers' thinking about the curriculum?

9. Looking at our curriculum as a whole, can we ascertain which areas of study are the least 'cohesive' and therefore need to be prioritised, ensuring relevant staff spend more time working on 'joining up' their curriculum?

10. Do the teachers in those areas of study mentioned in question 9 see the need for a shared vision for curriculum design and delivery?

11. Are teachers able to express the same detailed description of their curriculum aims and content as each other, not just for the classes they are teaching but also for other classes in the same area of focus within the school?

The next chapter looks at the first revolution: the outer circle of our curriculum wheel. Go to the very end of the book and you can see the 'pop out and keep' wheel that you can use for your revolutions, if you're fond of a gimmick.

2. Curriculum revolution: outer circle

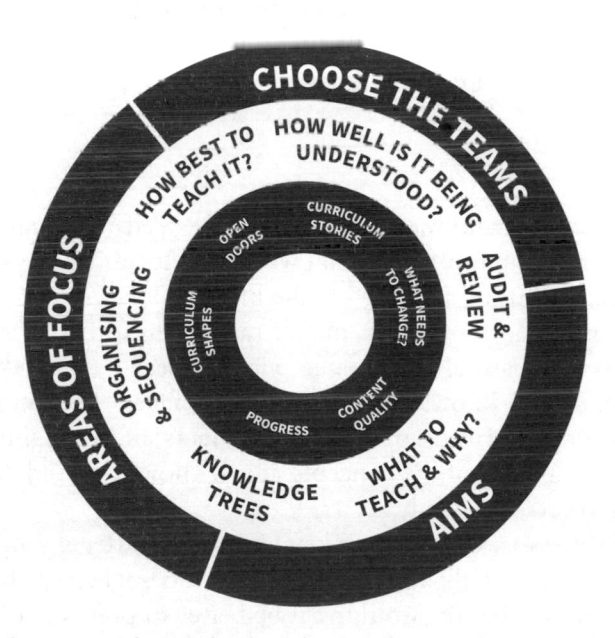

Although the curriculum wheel is designed in such a way that you can focus on each of the stages in whichever order suits you, it might be good, at first, to work from the outer circle to the inner circle and through each step consecutively. Therefore, it is envisaged that you will complete at least three revolutions before you go off-piste. While working through a revolution, you might wish to go forwards, backwards, return to something or fast-forward to a later stage depending on what the focus is at any particular time. But it is recommended that you go through each of the steps, to ensure any revisited steps are contained in the wider picture.

The outer revolution has three clear stages:

1. Aims.
2. Areas of focus.
3. Choose the teams.

You could start anywhere: it might be that the areas of focus are decided first, the curriculum teams are formed and then they decide their aims. It might be that the teams are formed, they decide their aims and then focus on areas of concern. For a whole-school approach, the senior leadership team might want to decide on the overall aims, choose which areas need focus and then identify who might best be involved in working on curriculum in those areas. In the first instance, it is recommended that you start with 'aims' and then follow the steps in a clockwise direction.

2a. Aims

Although the aims and the areas of focus are pretty self-explanatory in terms of curriculum improvement, I would like to emphasise some of the purposes served in the approach I take in this book.

The most important aim is one of making meaning. The idea is to create webs of meaning that enable pupils to learn and make sense of knowledge, of new knowledge, of conflicting ideas. They must venture into the world of forming opinions, arguments and thoughts based on sound understanding of the concepts, ideas, knowledge and debates that form the subjects they study.

Cohesiveness is, of course, a key aim. Once, after giving a talk on curriculum, I was challenged by someone who suggested that because the world was so chaotic, wouldn't it be better to prepare young people to live in that world by having them experience a chaotic curriculum? I responded that a chaotic mind is not the same as a chaotic world – we all need ways of understanding and ordering the world around us so that we can operate effectively within it. That doesn't mean we should ignore the possibility of ultimate meaninglessness – that we are all staring into the abyss and the nihilists have it right – but it is better to explain this through the study of Nietzsche than to use our curriculum design to underline the ultimate meaninglessness of being.

Yet it is a serious point and there is an argument against 'narrative'. However, the approach taken in this book builds on the idea of a complex narrative. In stories, there are often competing characters, themes, ideas and ways of seeing the world. A good curriculum, a rich curriculum, a well-designed curriculum is one that recognises these competing ways of interrogating the world. The world might sometimes seem chaotic and one of the jobs of curriculum is to help pupils find a way to cope, understand and make a difference, no matter how large or small.

A passionate and informed approach to curriculum design will have an impact on pupil outcomes. These outcomes should be, in the first instance, about wider issues than attainment scores. In other words, don't just aim for the kudos that higher grades in external exams might bring to the institution. Yes, results matter, but the overall quality of the education being offered matters far more. If you would rather an instrumentalist curriculum, focused entirely on grades, delivered results at the expense of a holistic and enriching education that frees pupils to know, think, play and enjoy the world – in other words, to flourish – then stop reading now.

Buy-in

In chapter 1 we looked at why collaboration is necessary. And although dissent can be a good thing, a shared understanding of *the process* is necessary. A couple of questions can help to ascertain how invested people are in the process. First, do they understand how each revolution is important to curriculum and to pedagogical development? Do they know that even those who are reticent about possible change have an important role to play? If not, it is necessary to create a shared understanding of the need for debate, dialogue and argument.

It is useful to ensure that the curriculum design process is tied into the school's professional development process, in order to show a shared institutional focus on the importance of curriculum. This also helps to create a culture of buy-in, where even those who are sceptical can see that their scepticism is a useful part of the ongoing dialogue. Bear in mind that professional scepticism can be a healthy response that can help to hone ideas and make ultimate decisions better. Whoever takes on the role of the sceptic is likely to change as different areas of focus emerge: yesterday's sceptic is tomorrow's enthusiast and vice versa. Beware the we-think of the enthusiastic team. The sceptical voice can be necessary and a 'critical friend' from outside the group can help, not just to solve problems but also to suggest them if no one else has!

Priorities for each curriculum revolution

How effective is the current curriculum? It is a good idea to begin the first curriculum revolution in a particular area with an audit, which can reveal the very issues you need to know about before you set about making changes. This audit should include a look at the effectiveness of the curriculum leadership and design up to this point. If you look at the middle wheel, you will see 'audit and review'. In this book, 'audit and review' is the last chapter (page 109), but, as the process is meant to be continuous, it could easily be the first. If you wish, check it out now: is there anything for you to use right away?

Once the areas of focus have been identified, it is important to ascertain if there will be any resistance to potential changes to the curriculum and its delivery. Curriculum change can be a fraught process, so any reticence should be aired, honestly and without judgement, from an early stage. These issues need to be taken on board. A revolution of the wheel might cause a literal revolution in the curriculum, and that can upset and alienate people if they do not feel their concerns have been listened to. Specifically, what this audit will offer is an insight into when change for change's sake is not what is required. Examining the strengths as well as the weaknesses of the status quo can often train the focus to where it is really needed.

It is important to explain the aim of the curriculum design process, how the school intends to use it, and how staff involvement is key, not only to improved pupil outcomes and a better-quality curriculum but also to make clear where further professional development is required. This can be in terms of content knowledge, understanding how the curriculum hangs together, and any pedagogical changes that may be required.

This depends very much on how curriculum design has been

done before in your institution. In some schools, where it has been completely left to departments or individual teachers, there might be some trepidation about putting design on a more formal footing. Put staff members' minds at rest: this is about them thinking more deeply about the quality of their curriculum, as a team, and taking control of when and where to change things, safe in the knowledge that the changes are intended to make their jobs more fulfilling and the learning of their pupils more complete. And although 'If it ain't broke, don't fix it' is a good rule of thumb, the best curriculum is one that is adaptable. Changes, no matter how minor, can improve things if they are made thoughtfully and diligently. This process should help.

2b. Areas of focus

The areas of focus can **range** from some form of multidisciplinary focus – for example, essay-writing or graphs – to a more qualitative focus on texts: are they of sufficient quality? The focus might be on co-curricular or extracurricular work. What opportunities and entitlements are pupils offered? These will include clubs and societies in the school, the productions and sports, exhibitions and recitals, guest speakers and trips. The main areas of focus, however, will probably be the subject areas and/or disciplines. In the first instance, it is probably a good idea to focus on the subjects – get this right and much else can follow. This is true for secondary as well as primary but, of course, it is not necessarily straightforward.

Professional development is an essential part of the process. There might be limitations in the curriculum that are down to staff confidence and/or competence and how secure they feel their knowledge is in a given area of focus. It might be worth being clear: first let's try to design the best possible curriculum and then, as part of the process, identify any professional development and/or staffing requirements that might be required to make the desired changes. If these changes can't happen straight away, that is not a reason for not planning for them in the future. There is also an issue of trust here: do the staff feel confident enough to suggest what their own developmental needs might be in the context of potential curriculum changes?

The division of the curriculum into certain areas should be revisited as time goes by. One of the first questions to ask is: what subjects do we teach and why? This question can lead you into interesting areas – one of the most obvious might be the realisation that it can't be answered adequately beyond 'So the kids can get the exam results they need' or 'Because of staffing' or 'Because we've always taught these subjects'. Although these are perfectly reasonable, pragmatic answers, in many people's eyes they don't inspire a sense of meaning and purpose. Think of a school that offers very little in the way of the arts or sport; subjects are squeezed into ever smaller silos, or into carousels, to make way for the big, important subjects. What messages are we sending about the relative status of subjects, the quality of the knowledge that is offered and therefore the ability of those subject teachers to really offer a worthwhile experience? A critical look at the school's overall curriculum offer from the point of view of each area of study might bring some uncomfortable facts to the surface, but all the better that they are addressed.

A similar question could be asked: what co-curricular/extracurricular opportunities are on offer and why? It might be that these activities are mainly focused on exam catch-up and support. They might revolve around sports day and a school play. They might be clubs based on teachers' passions. Or perhaps the school does not offer any because the staff are so overworked. Whatever the answers, how can the aims and the areas of focus match up? Having lofty aims and pointing to areas of focus where these aims are being achieved is better than seeking excuses for what is already being done.

All staff need to understand how this iterative process for curriculum design will impact on school meetings, resources and lesson delivery. Each revolution of the curriculum wheel requires time, thought and resources. Ensure the requisite time, space and resources are set aside for formal and informal work on curriculum – perhaps an hour or more a week for focused work and opportunities for an 'open doors' approach (see chapter 8) that allows more informal meetings to take place.

There are two major ways of dealing with curriculum design. First, a **reactive focus** on things that are going wrong and, second, a **proactive focus** that seeks to alleviate the need for the former.

Reactive focus

Curriculum effectiveness needs to be monitored continually, with teachers picking up on any unexpected gaps in pupil knowledge. When these gaps can be attributed to individual pupils missing chunks of curriculum time, there should be an awareness that this missed time was not dealt with adequately. When it is clear the gaps are shared among a whole cohort, or among a significant number of pupils, this indicates an overall design issue that must be logged and dealt with, hence the need for regular curriculum meetings. When the gaps are shared by a specific group within the cohort then the reason needs to be ascertained: what is it that these pupils have in common? There may be an issue of special needs, or perhaps the issue is that a teacher has not taught that part of the curriculum effectively, or at all.

This can be summed up in the phrase 'the responsive curriculum' and is one of the major reasons why I think the job of curriculum design is never finished. Sometimes things don't work quite the way they are expected to. There are also a large number of variables, including different children, teachers and the ever-changing cultural milieu in which we find ourselves – a pandemic being one of the more extreme examples of this.

Formally and informally, teachers need to be able to talk about and look for solutions to any problems that *might* be down to the curriculum design having significant issues. When there are gaps, can these be plugged somehow, both in the here and now and also with those pupils who are currently learning (or *not* learning) that 'bit' of the curriculum where the problems are deemed to have occurred?

This is an assessment issue, not seeing assessment as a way to differentiate children from each other but as a way to judge how well a curriculum is designed and delivered. Whatever the issue might be, there is no time like the present to ensure it is dealt with – and dealt with, I must emphasise, in a constructive and collegiate way.

Proactive focus

It's not – and shouldn't be – all firefighting. Features of the curriculum revolution must be revisited over time, in order to build a fluid and regular commitment to improvement through our curriculum design teams and leadership – in line with changes in individual subjects as well as local, national and international impacts on curriculum content.

It is essential to identify the areas of curriculum that are the specific focus of each revolution. (This could be parts of the curriculum, subject areas or any number of areas that need focus, according to the school's own way of organising the curriculum and its leadership.) What are the priorities? Why are they the priorities? Who should be on the design teams? When should the process be completed? Where and when should people meet?

And *how* should the process be completed? Well, this can be achieved via use of the wheel – our tool for curriculum revolutions.

2c. Choose the teams

Once the areas of focus have been decided, who should be on the design team? This is usually obvious – for example, the members of the department – but this can be very difficult to organise. The things that get in the way are departments that are too large or too small, have too many temporary or non-specialist staff, or too many staff who are set in their ways. It is easy for staff who are of the latter persuasion to pay lip service to curriculum design changes and then go back to what they have always done once the classroom door is closed. It is also easy for new members of staff to say, 'Give me the lesson plans and schemes of work, or whatever you've got, and I'll just deliver that.' The point of the curriculum design team is to bring about a cohesive curriculum design that doesn't just look good on paper, or on a website, but is actually taught in a cohesive manner – and this means it needs maximum buy-in.

Who makes up the design team, therefore, is crucial to the success of not just the design but also its delivery. It is also important that the team members realise they have to work together, rather than delegate work to be done separately. Curriculum cohesion requires deep knowledge of how the curriculum connects and so demands a shared organisational mind.

Collaborative curriculum design should not be a process that produces contented platitudes like 'We are all singing from the same hymn sheet'. Disagreement is a healthy part of collaboration. The aim should be to produce an atmosphere – a culture – in which passionate disagreement can be harnessed in interesting and perhaps surprising ways in order to create a cohesive and vibrant curriculum. Although everyone will have to compromise – at least until the debates are able to rage again – it is the rich quality of airing and thinking through disagreement that makes the curriculum one everybody can buy into. A curriculum that is nodded through by a tired and despondent staff, wanting to go home, is never going to be as good as one that has fire in its belly.

To help work through disagreements or, indeed, stir things up, it can be a good idea for each team to have a 'critical friend'. Someone who can sit outside the decision-making process but can advise, cajole, help out and enable better decisions to be made, as well as question those that might not be the best decisions in the circumstances. This is an obvious role for a curriculum leader, who can provide an overview of how the curriculum design process in the school is progressing as a whole.

Organisational questions

Here are some questions that may help you to structure the team. Feel free to add your own and to disregard some or all of the following.

1. Who is in the team?
2. Is there an overall team leader?
3. Do different team members take the lead in different parts of the curriculum? What are these parts and who is responsible for leading each one?
4. What will we do to resolve areas of dispute and reach agreement?[2]
5. How will we know if we are making good decisions?
6. Is enough time being allocated to curriculum design?[3]
7. Should we appoint a critical friend?

---

2   Agreement means a shared understanding of the aims and methods of good curriculum design, not some sort of false consensus. An argumentative, passionate team who listen and try to understand a range of perspectives are likely to come up with a better curriculum than a team who long for a quiet life and scowl at those who rock the boat.

3   This question refers not just to how many hours are allocated but also to the times of day: do meetings happen at the end of the day or term, when everyone is exhausted? The teams need time for focused attention and thought. If there is too little time, staff might go off on their own or in small groups to work on one or two areas, but this usually leads to gaps in knowledge and a level of incoherence.

Review questions for the critical friend

1. How do we know whether the teams are effective and their contributions are improving curriculum connectivity?
2. What resources do the teams need to do their job effectively? How do we know?
3. What might be the next steps?
4. Is the process working well? How do we know? What changes, if any, should be made to the teams and/or the process?
5. Have we gone up any blind alleys?
6. What decisions have we made and who needs to know? *(The critical friend and curriculum team might need to consider the best staff members to communicate the progress being made.)*
7. What impact might the work have on teacher practice? What do we need to put in place to enable a positive and successful impact?
8. What impact might the changes have on our pupils? How do we ensure this will be overwhelmingly positive? How do we measure and make sure the impact on pupil performance outcomes is also positive?

Curriculum culture supports the teams

How best can the school create structures that allow staff to talk about their curriculum, formally and informally? Time, space and a positive culture are necessary to allow this. The structures must not just be formal, because 'water-cooler' opportunities to share feedback and ideas offer the most immediate curriculum review. A positive curriculum culture should be encouraged by the school as part of the process of curriculum revolutions – not everything has to be minuted and formally acted upon.

But how can best practice be discussed and shared across the school if not everything is minuted? This might suggest that minuting and reporting everything works as a method of communication. Of course, it does for specific things: simple messages about someone doing something particular at a certain time, or about an 'order' with which you must comply, are effectively communicated by an email or by direct instruction at a meeting. However, curriculum is different. It involves conversations between multiple people. It evolves. And though specifics must be arrived at and carried out, getting to these specifics takes time and a shift in culture. This shift in culture is best described in the term 'curriculum conversations'.

Curriculum conversations enhance the teams

What capacity and resources do teachers need in order to engage in curriculum conversations? How do you know? How do you know the quality of curriculum consistency across departments/subjects (and other areas of curriculum organisation and delivery that the school deems important)? How does this impact the membership of the team? How do you understand the quality of conversations that need to be had in curriculum areas (subjects and/or other areas that the school deems important) in which you have little or no expertise? How can you be sure that the decisions regarding curriculum changes are being made by agreement throughout a team? How do you know your teams' ways of working are effective?

The first thing each team could do is to get some idea of what they agree would constitute a 'good' curriculum at this stage in the development of their work. They should also decide how they can encourage useful formal and informal curriculum conversations that could enable them to keep developing and strengthening their curriculum knowledge, cohesiveness, progress and design thinking, as well as how to reach decisions.

Discussion

- Looking at the curriculum wheel, what are our priorities for the development of the necessary curriculum conversations? How do we know they are the right priorities?
- How does the curriculum wheel model for curriculum improvement compare and contrast with what has been done up to now? This might point to the need for an audit (see chapter 10).
- What might be the impact of a model of continual curriculum design in terms of teacher time and efficiency? A more efficient curriculum might lead to time being saved in the classroom. However, it will require more time for teachers to work together collaboratively and regularly on curriculum design.

- How well prepared are the people who might be involved in the curriculum design process? Do they require specific professional development before the process begins?
- What needs might people have in terms of time, space and resourcing (including any specific training requirements)?
- How can we set up a programme of formal and informal conversations around the areas highlighted in the curriculum wheel, within a number of subject/disciplinary areas?
- How long should the first revolution take? Do we need to set a deadline for completion or just let the process take its course, checking in and asking for ongoing reporting on its progress?

3. Curriculum revolution: middle and inner circles

The middle and inner circles are designed to be the main focus for curriculum design. Each revolution will take you further along a sustainable and cohesive approach to curriculum design and enable you to build on previous work.

The middle circle has six main 'stops':

1. What to teach and why?
2. Knowledge trees.
3. Organising and sequencing.
4. How best to teach it?
5. How well is it being understood?
6. Audit and review.

And the inner circle offers six more-focused stages:

1. Content quality.
2. Progress.
3. Curriculum shapes.
4. Open doors.
5. Curriculum stories.
6. What needs to change?

Although the intention is for you to follow the stages in the above order for the first revolution, you might wish to start at 'audit and review'. As I wrote in chapter 2, the curriculum wheel is designed in such a way that you can focus on each of the stages in whichever order suits you. While working through a revolution, you might wish to go forwards, go backwards, return to something or fast-forward to a later stage, depending on what the focus is at any particular time.

The inner circle relates to the middle circle and can give you a more nuanced or focused approach. It can be used alongside the middle circle or as a revolution in its own right.

The table below gives a brief description of each stage on the middle and inner circles. The following chapters will look at these 'stops' in more detail, offering ideas you might want to take on board and actions you might wish to take.

	Middle circle	**Inner circle**
Revolution first stop (on the initial revolution, you might wish to visit stop six before this stop)	**What to teach and why?** Curriculum content: what do we have to teach? What are we currently teaching? Why are we teaching what we are teaching?	**Content quality.** Is our curriculum any good and how do we know?
Revolution second stop	**Knowledge trees.** What knowledge and skills should an educated person in this area of focus need in order to understand this subject and be able to carry out tasks with a good degree of competence?	**Progress.** What does the process of getting from a relative novice to relative expert look like in this subject area?
Revolution third stop	**Organising and sequencing.** What are the optimum ways to organise the curriculum content to aid understanding? This is the essence of good curriculum design.	**Curriculum shapes.** Curriculum shapes and thinking about connectivity can help to organise and sequence the knowledge and skills.

Revolution fourth stop	**How best to teach it?** How we go about teaching the content impacts on the skills and competencies we are trying to engender. We need to think about what we are asking pupils to produce and the progress we expect them to make from something akin to novices to something approaching experts.	**Open doors.** How do we ensure an 'open door' policy, wherein our classrooms are always open to co-working, reviewing, supporting and learning from each other?
Revolution fifth stop	**How well is it being understood?** A curriculum doesn't just exist on a website or in a booklet. It is most importantly understood as a way of thinking about the world that exists in a pupil's mind at a given time.	**Curriculum stories.** A good way to review curriculum cohesiveness is to ask teachers, pupils and other 'stakeholders' their curriculum stories. Take them on journeys along their curriculum webs, their schema, to 'tell' their stories. The more consistent these stories are, the better, and they should also contain interesting perspectives – the subjective part is revealing and important. We should be far less interested in whether they are 'enjoying' the curriculum and more interested in how they are understanding it.
Revolution sixth stop (and possibly the first stop on the initial revolution)	**Audit and review.** This is self-explanatory, although it is important that this revolution is seen not as an end to curriculum design but a beginning for potential changes.	**What needs to change?** This should be a list of content and tangible areas of concern, rather than more 'woolly' areas that, although they might be important, may not lead anywhere.

4. What to teach and why?

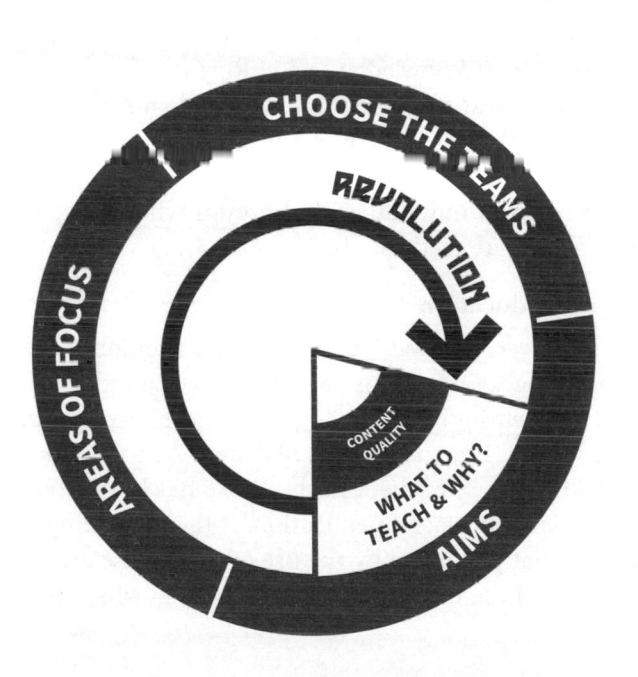

Middle circle: what to teach and why?

What is the most suitable content in terms of our ethos and aims, and how the content links to local, national and international concerns including government legislation, or to relevant issues at a given time? How much shared understanding is there about what is in the curriculum and why it is included? How detailed is the shared understanding of what is taught and how it links to other areas of the curriculum? Can our team of intrepid curriculum designers agree on the most important content to teach in terms of knowledge, skills and competencies?

This knowledge might be dictated by a national or local curriculum, as well as other relevant local and international, cultural, philosophical, historical, social and scientific ideas – for example, climate change or a need to tell a 'national story'. One way to establish the most important knowledge within a curriculum area is to think about the 'big ideas' – foundational concepts that provide the context that helps us to frame and focus on what we wish to teach.

It is also essential to consider the physical, social and mental capabilities of those you teach and how to make the curriculum open for as many as possible. If knowledge and culture are for everyone then we must consider how best to make them accessible for everyone. This can have an impact on the choices you make and on how you accommodate all that you want to achieve. It might be worth thinking about how the curriculum is open to individuals and groups who are neurodiverse or have a range of special needs or abilities.

Knowledge-rich education

Knowledge is power. The best that has been thought, said and done. Powerful knowledge. Cultural literacy. Cultural capital.

Often cited, seemingly interchangeably, these concepts have definite parentage: in order, Francis Bacon, Matthew Arnold, Michael Young, ED Hirsch and Pierre Bourdieu. Each phrase has been used to describe a 'knowledge-rich' approach to education. If they are being used in your school, decide what you mean by the use of the phrase and how it works in your context. These descriptors help us in the 'why' and guide us in the 'what'.

Knowing as belonging, imagining and creating

Belonging is central to many 'nationalist' approaches to curriculum design. The idea of nation-building and cultural cohesion can be important, certainly at times of conflict. After the Second World War, the Allies set about trying to 'educate' – or to 'de-Nazify' – the populations of countries where the far-right ideology had taken root. Former and latter curriculum approaches were shaped around an idea of 'belonging', but what changes is the understanding of *what we belong to*.

Is the knowledge we want to teach indicative of a local, national or international ideal? A mix? How would these different foci change our content? Is the idea of 'belonging' to something key to our values?

Creative subjects are not just about reproducing something that has been done before, but also about allowing pupils to go beyond the boundary of what is known and/or familiar. This involves getting to know radical and/or revolutionary works from the past or present and allowing pupils the space to produce new knowledge.

Knowledge that is completely new in every way permits us no 'way in', because we have nothing by which to anchor it. This is why what is taught before – which becomes the foundation of what follows – is so important. The avant-garde exists to challenge the 'known', to shock us with the new. Of course, if it was totally new it would be rejected – there must be enough that is 'known' within the new to help us accept it.

If children have a 'way in', probably cultural, to a subject then they can see it as 'familiar' or at least as something they can accept as being worthy of study. This knowledge can be understood as a way of 'belonging' to something.

Beyond 'belonging' is the power of 'imagining'. New ways of thinking, of being, of creating new things. This type of knowing involves creating something new and yet feeling it as familiar – knowing something because it feels right. This is how, when creating something new, we judge whether it is any good. Intuition is brought into play. 'I'll know it when it's good' is a judgement call, associated with an 'educated palate'.

This form of knowing is developed in many subjects: in the interplay between feelings, facts and judgements; in arguing your corner; in knowing when enough paint has been marshalled to represent the topic of the painting; in trusting your own judgements; in knowing when something is 'just right'.

Whose knowledge?

A curriculum is a cultural artefact. A 'national curriculum' will often focus on a 'national character' or 'national values'; it often has 'aims and objectives' that the nation deems to be important. There are other competing interest groups: 'local curricula' might be desired, or oppositional curricula if the state is deemed to be beyond the pale – this might be one reason for home-educating, for example. Some religious groups might want their own forms of curriculum: some want more traditional values while others are more progressive. Managerialist technocrats might want gleaming schools full of computers; dreary traditionalists might want chalk and talk, exams and tests. A curriculum is inevitably tied to 'culture', which can lead people to ask whose culture it should reflect. 'Whose knowledge?' is the way this question is often asked.

Culture is contestable. Once something has been chosen for inclusion in a curriculum, there could be a thousand voices suggesting that the wrong choice has been made and that something else should have been chosen instead. Sometimes the argument is made that the knowledge has been included owing to biases among teachers, who belong to a certain society at a given time. For a Marxist, the choices might be about power: knowledge of the powerful is chosen because they have the economic clout to naturalise their cultural tastes and values as 'common sense' truths. A liberal humanist might have a counterargument stating that what is valued is less about power relations and is more reflective of longevity owing to intrinsic value and/or truth. Whichever argument you believe, the question 'Whose knowledge?' is often asked in debates about curriculum content.

The problem with the question is that it gives the impression that culture or knowledge can be 'owned'. Certainly, people can copyright work, put a patent on an invention, or claim something to be their 'intellectual property'. But the nature of knowledge and culture is such that ownership can't always be claimed, certainly not by a 'group of people'. On receiving Norway's 2019 Holberg Prize, the cultural historian Professor Paul Gilroy said:

> *We [have] to try to think about culture in a slightly different way than the one which asserts it's primarily tied to territory, to fixity, to soil, to belonging. We [have] to accommodate the flows, the migrations, the transformations, the mixtures, the movements, that [make] culture anew.*[4]

---

4   Holberg Prize. (2019) 'The 2019 Holberg Conversation with Paul Gilroy' (video), YouTube, https://youtu.be/PBntPdPcQes

To suggest that knowledge belongs to a group means accepting that a group is sufficiently fixed and similar over time and place, and that the boundaries around both are hermetically sealed. Just as human beings are mobile, so the culture through which we get to know the world is fluid. All things are mixed up and nothing remains the same. Tradition is important for identity and stability, but it is always coming up against new challenges, something that is recognised by many institutions over time as they adapt in order to remain relevant in the modern world. The idea of 'nation' is important and something that many schools feel it is important to represent, to bind us together through rights, responsibilities and obligations. A certain pride in nation can help to build a vibrant community, but a patriotic celebration of togetherness is different to a belief in cultural superiority.

Whether the idea is of a superior national/regional culture or of a 'master race', the notion that some kind of cultural superiority has accompanied a class, race or religion throughout time is just plain wrong. This argument has been used for sinister purposes time and again. Despite the claims of cultural elitists, there is no 'knowledge' that provides evidence of a superior group of people throughout time. On close inspection, it is difficult to nail down culture as being owned by any 'group' of human beings, because culture and groups of human beings are products of intermixture. This anti-essentialist viewpoint is the same for all claims of cultural ownership.

As Gilroy wrote, in the case of race:

> An ... area of political difficulty comes into view when the voguish language of absolute cultural difference associated with the ontological essentialist standpoint provides an embarrassing link between the practice of blacks who comprehend racial politics through it and the activities of their foresworn opponents — the ethnic absolutists of the racist right — who approach the complex dynamics of race, nationality, and ethnicity through a similar set of pseudo-precise, culturalist equations.[5]

There are calls nowadays to 'decolonise the curriculum'. However, it is not always clear what this might mean in practice. We sometimes see

---

5   Gilroy, P. (1993) *The Black Atlantic: modernity and double consciousness*, Harvard University Press, p.34

tokenistic approaches, especially around events such as Black History Month and the adding of a non-white author or two to the literature offer of a school. Others go further and questions around identity and 'whiteness' are added to the curriculum, accompanied by phrases such as 'white fragility' and 'white privilege'. In his book *Against Decolonisation*, Olúfẹ́mi Táíwò writes:

> ... *the confusion that I identify with the decolonisation discourse is the almost indiscriminate deployment of it to address anything and everything ... My hope is that drawing attention to the catch-all use of this might cool our ardour for throwing 'decolonisation' at whatever ails our discussion in philosophy and culture more broadly.*[6]

We should not fall into the trap of equating a class or a race with one viewpoint, believing that by diversifying the curriculum's authors, artists and scientists we have represented something profound about the ownership of knowledge. Instead of implying that knowledge and identity are joined and fixed, we need to explore with our curriculum content the complexity of our arts, languages, sciences, humanities, technologies, philosophies, ideologies; the changing nature of the culture(s) through which we make meaning in the world.

As the historian David Olusoga puts it: 'One of the problems we have is that phrases like "decolonise the curriculum" ... it's just so easy to dismiss or to mischaracterise that phrase ... "Make the curriculum tell everyone's stories" ... is actually what you're saying.'[7]

This makes more sense. By bringing a range of perspectives to bear we have a broader curriculum and one that encourages pupils to begin to develop their own tastes, opinions and thoughts. In other words, to begin to find meaning for themselves in the world(s) we introduce to them.

Perspectivism

To rise to the need to 'tell everyone's stories', we should look to the curriculum to bring a variety of perspectives to the subjects in hand. We

---

6   Táíwò, O. (2022) *Against Decolonisation: taking African agency seriously*, Hurst, p.58

7   The British Library. (2020) 'David Olusoga in conversation: black history matters' (video), YouTube, https://youtu.be/zDO1bdT47Rc

can get aspects of the curriculum to argue and/or converse with other parts. This diversity of perspective is likely to include a variety of different voices, rather than representing one sex, race, class or sexuality with a particular cultural product or 'type' of knowledge. Seeking out different perspectives leads to an enriched cultural experience; it underlines that knowledge and culture is for everyone. One of the arguments for the long study of a broad range of subjects is how it brings a wide range of different perspectives to our meaning-making.

Rather than asking 'Whose knowledge?', we can see knowledge as shared and culture as fluid; a means for rich communication and conversation.

Hierarchies of knowledge

There are different hierarchies when it comes to knowledge. Threshold concepts might be considered more important, or organising principles, ideas, ideologies, frameworks, etc. All offer the possibility of encapsulating how knowledge works. Knowledge is not in isolation; it is not just 'facts' or lists of things that everyone should know. Rather, knowledge works by connecting things up: new pieces of knowledge are made sense of by how they fit with other pieces of knowledge.

Knowledge builds on knowledge and skills grow. These two ideas are important. If we think of knowledge as working in a schematic way – as weaving a web – and skills as building on a trajectory from novice to expert, we see how our curriculum might take shape. What are the big themes and ideas in our area of focus?

Connections

The secret of good curriculum design is actually an 'open' secret – a good curriculum connects things together. We will explore how to make it connect in chapters 6 and 7. But at this stage, it is worth thinking about what knowledge 'connects' other knowledge. What skills and competencies can be developed to help pupils navigate the subject? Do our pupils understand how knowledge is knitted together? Can they tell our curriculum stories and look for links that we have taught them either implicitly and/or explicitly?

For curriculum design, skills that are weaved into the curriculum must be seen as vital to the pupil's development in the subject, which means progress matters. Think of the pupil learning to play the violin: in her first lesson she is not expected to be able to play Beethoven's violin concertos; instead, she might be taught how to hold the violin under her chin and how to hold the bow. In her first driving lesson, the pupil is not given the keys and told to get on with it. A three-year-old is not given an adult-sized racing bike and a yellow jersey and dropped off in France for 'Le Tour'.

Discussion

- What is the most suitable content in terms of our ethos and aims, and how it links to local, national and international concerns including government legislation?
- How much shared understanding is in the school of what is in the curriculum and why?
- How detailed is the shared understanding of what is taught and how it links to other areas of the curriculum?
- Can we agree on the most important content to teach in terms of knowledge, skills and competencies?
- What guides us in our choices? Is this 'guidance' useful and sufficient, or do we need to focus further?
- If there are areas of disagreement about what to include in the curriculum, how best can we resolve them?
- How do we ensure that we aim high for all and make knowledge accessible to all?
- How do we know that our teachers' knowledge is sufficient to teach this content well?
- How shared is the commitment to the qualitative richness of curriculum content within the team? What are the dissenting voices saying? Are the points they are making pertinent to the issues that are of concern? Can their opinions be incorporated in some way, or is the 'greater good' served by noting their differing opinions but continuing with the 'other' viewpoints? Can the critical voices acquiesce to this in the short and/or medium/long term?

- Is 'belonging' to something important to our choices?
- What are the 'big' themes and ideas in our area of focus?
- How do we ensure that we reflect a range of perspectives on the topics we intend to cover?
- How best to use existing resources and textbooks? Do any of these materials need updating or need to be used in different ways?
- Might it be useful to compare with what other schools are teaching?
- How might the individual content choices we make impact on the overall curriculum?
- What expertise do we have? Do any of us need professional development in terms of subject knowledge in any of the areas discussed? Can this CPD be provided in house or through outside agencies/resources?

Inner circle: content quality

'Is it any good?' is an important question. There are two ways to look at this. First, is the content good in terms of satisfying some commitment to teach the subject? Does it satisfy some basic criteria? Second, and the more important question to answer, is it *qualitatively* good? This does not mean it has to be 'the best', but it does need some directional aptitude towards being 'good' or 'truthful' or 'right'. And although not everything has to be of the same quality, is there enough that might satisfy subject demands to show, inform and explain what the best in a subject might be or could be, even if this is perhaps more difficult for pupils to understand or relate to? Of course, knowledge is not experienced 'alone', so it's important to think about it in context – more on this later.

This doesn't always mean it *is* difficult. Some simple things can be, arguably, 'the best' – famously, a pile of bricks gets exhibited in the Tate gallery in London. The reasoning, however, might be complex. This is a subjective judgement, in most cases, so it might cause arguments rather than passive agreement. Better the former than the latter. This judgement should not just be about individual pieces of information or nuggets of knowledge – which will, importantly, vary in quality – but also about the general, the sum of its parts. Is the overall education that this curriculum provides any good? Justify it.

What we deem to be good is not a list of things, but must be seen in the round. How does it all fit together? Does our curriculum give a true representation of our subject and/or area of focus? Is it a good grounding that allows pupils to navigate the subject away from the classroom, away from their teacher? At what level? Bear in mind that pupils will arrive and leave our curriculum at different times and therefore with different levels of knowledge and abilities to use that knowledge, so we want to ensure they are able to take an element of interest and move beyond our teaching. Maybe they will go to a concert, speak a native language in another country, read a science report in the paper, or listen to a doctor or a mechanic after an MOT (human or car) and realise they have a way in to understand the experience.

How good is good enough? How could it be better?

Discussion

- How do we know this is the right and the best content for our pupils to learn?
- Do our choices allow pupils to decide what they think might be the best, allowing them to develop as thinkers who are beginning to foster their own values, tastes and ideas?
- Will our curriculum offer specific challenges or difficulties to certain pupils? If so, what should we do?
- In terms of the quality of curriculum content, focus some of the questions on: why this and not this?
- Do we know what is the best practice in curriculum content and do we have any interesting examples we can draw upon?

5. Knowledge trees

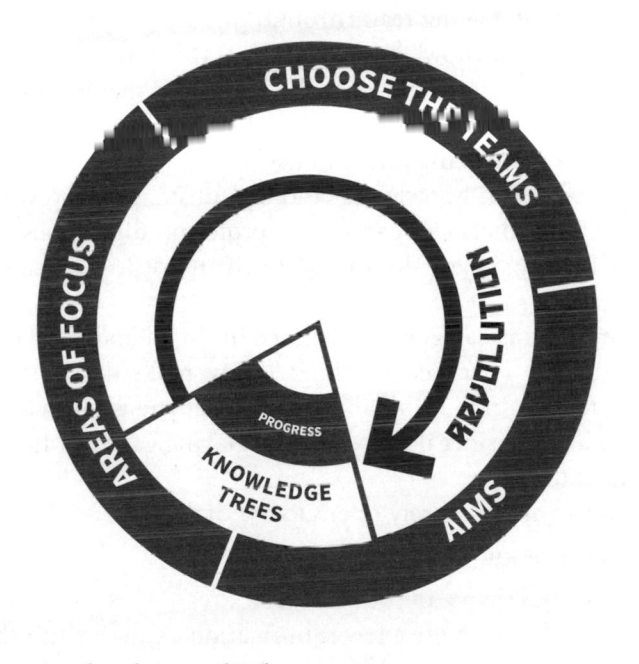

Middle circle: knowledge trees

Having thought about what to teach and why, the next step is to consider how to *organise* the content you wish to teach. This might involve rethinking some of the content ideas you have come up with, so be prepared to change your mind. Curriculum design is, inevitably, iterative: decisions are made and remade and remade.

Each decision can be thought of as provisional; it is revised through each revolution.

Organising what you want to teach

Remember, not everything in this chapter will be relevant to the stage you are at. You are always free to accept or reject any of the ideas.

The first step in organising the knowledge is to think about the broad knowledge categories that the content might fit into. This focus will help you not only to decide where things might belong in your curriculum, but also to think about how things might be best understood by your pupils.

It might be that, having read through this chapter, you don't see any need to categorise the knowledge you teach at this stage, or indeed ever. It might be that your school stipulates the categories that you are expected to use and therefore you are trying to find a way to make them work for you. Whether you are being asked to use 'the best that has been thought and said' or 'powerful knowledge' and/or 'substantive and disciplinary knowledge', these edicts can cause very profound difficulties if the way you are teaching a subject doesn't quite fit in with these categories of knowledge.

Look through the categories discussed in this chapter and maybe add some of your own. Then decide which, if any, make the most sense and are most useful. Begin to think about how what you want to teach might be organised and consider if there are any glaring gaps in what you have, so far, decided to teach.

Questions to ask to merely open up the dialogue:

- What sorts of knowledge do we teach?
- What is the shape of our subject area? This rudimentary question can have quite a few ramifications. Curriculum shapes are discussed in chapter 7, but at this stage it is worth thinking about how the curriculum you currently teach works: is it tall and thin? Does it progress like a ladder from one thing to another? Or is it wider and more shallow, with lots of things that can be learned alongside each other and, perhaps, more easily changed, in that one thing can be removed or replaced in the curriculum without toppling the whole house of cards?

- Are we catering for skills and/or competencies?
- How might thinking about different types of knowledge impact on curriculum design, pedagogy and assessment?
- How can our pupils best make progress?

Fields, subjects and domains

These are all descriptions of 'areas of study'. Whether you think of the area of study as a discipline, subject, art, terrain or field might impact on how you separate it from other areas. Moving from one field to another seems simpler than going from one discipline to another, at least metaphorically. Does it matter what you call your area of study? Maybe, maybe not. Some might exist within another: fields of knowledge might refer to broad areas within a discipline. We can 'examine the terrain' within a discipline, too.

Categorising knowledge

Aristotle divided knowledge in various ways. One of the most useful, for curriculum design, is the following: theoretical knowledge (*theoria* in Greek), practical knowledge (*praxis*) and productive knowledge (*poiēsis*). Here, praxis refers to doing things in the world – for example, making arguments, or political and ethical decisions, individually or collectively.

Categories are only useful if they help to explain the subject and how it is organised to pupils, or help to design how the curriculum might be taught. If the categories are useful then use them – if not, don't.

When considering what to teach and why, we might get into questions about epistemology and ontology. This is the philosophy behind the content we have begun to look at. If we ask, 'What is needed to get through an exam?' we will have a limited, perfunctory curriculum that might get some good results but won't necessarily leave pupils knowing much about a subject. If we guide questions about content around ideas of 'quality' – famously, 'the best that has been thought and said' – then we begin to explore in greater depth what is 'good' to learn.

However, 'the best' is always up for grabs; it changes as time goes by and is such a subjective notion in so many subjects that it can be all but impossible to pin down. This is not to say that it shouldn't be discussed. Making lists of 'the best' in a subject can be a useful part of the process of curriculum design, owing to the conversations it unleashes. A good question to ask might then be, 'What knowledge does an educated person in this area of study need in order to understand this subject, so that they can think and discuss widely about it, can agree and disagree with their peers and their teachers, and even get involved in discussion about what, in this subject, the best might be?' In some subjects, knowledge is less certain than others. In science and art, the pursuit of truth and/or beauty might be wildly different things and rely on different ways of knowing and applying knowledge.

If we look at knowledge as isolated chunks that need to be learned, it is difficult to make sense of a subject, let alone how that subject might link to other subjects. And yet, so often I see schools teaching a subject as though it is actually about isolated chunks of knowledge. For example, an English class might study 'one damn text after another': a short story this half-term, a novel the next and a play after that, without any clue about how these things come together (or not). Rather than following lists of 'stuff' to learn, we should be teaching knowledge that connects and builds, allowing children freedom to roam. This freedom comes only from a properly constructed curriculum: a web of knowledge.

Branches of knowledge

Instead of isolated chunks or lists, we begin to look at how knowledge 'connects'. Knowledge trees can help us to do this. Think of the trunk as 'our subject' and then consider what the branches of knowledge might be.

In my own subject, drama, the first two branches are 'theory' and 'practical'. These categories of knowledge impact on many things that directly affected how my pupils experienced their learning: on their progress (some were all-rounders, some were better at theory, some were better at practical); on equipment and technology; on rooming; on assessment. For practical, we used a workshop space; for theory, a seminar room or classroom. For practical, pupils got changed in the changing rooms and prepared for a predominantly physical exploration of the subject; in theory, with pens, notebooks or laptops at the ready, pupils engaged with knowledge in a different way. In terms of progress, sometimes the two branches explored the same topics; at other times, they veered away from each other. The way the knowledge was organised affected the overall understanding of the subject and how pupils engaged with it.

It might be that the knowledge trees illustrated on the following pages are useful. Mixing and matching from various trees might help you on your way. Your own trees or branches might be added to the mix. Whatever helps you to make your connections and organise your knowledge usefully.

Theoretical knowledge and practical knowledge

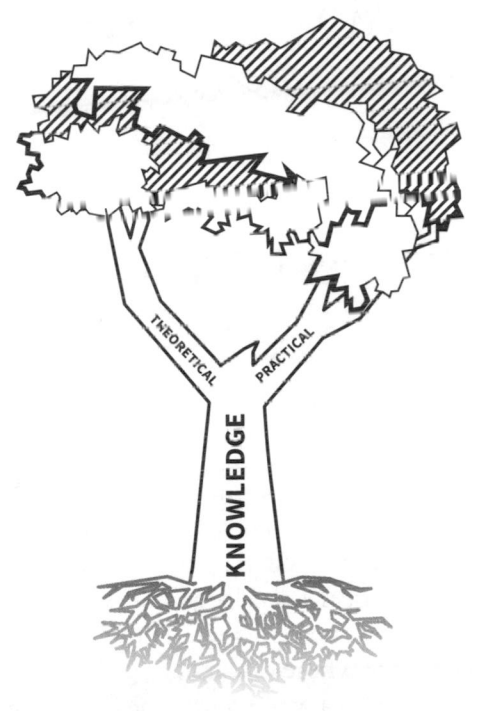

A forerunner of the knowledge vs skills distinction is perhaps the line drawn between philosophical or scientific knowledge and empirical or practical knowledge, with the former learned from books and the latter from experience. The university vs the university of life. Does this distinction exist in your subject? Is it a useful one in order to categorise knowledge? This distinction can work for arts subjects: often you hear of arts subjects being divided into theory and practical.

Knowledge and skills

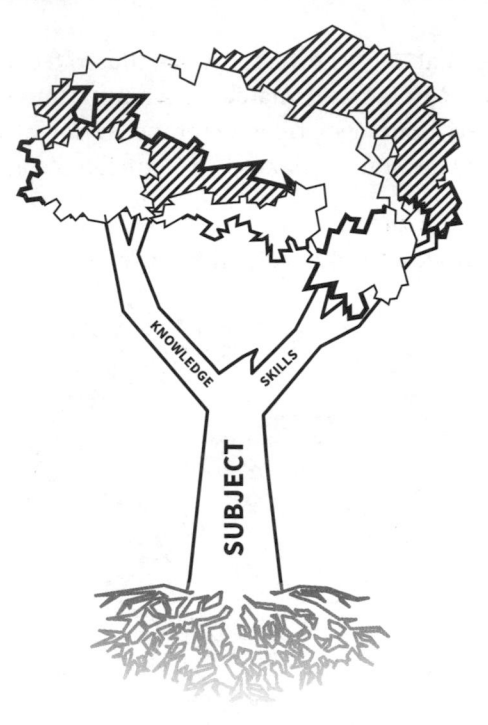

The difference between knowledge and skills is difficult to pin down: do we 'know' how to ride a bicycle or are we 'skilful' at riding a bike? Do we know how to study or do we have the necessary study skills to be a good student? Practical knowledge and skills seem to be akin to doing, to action, whereas knowledge on its own might be more akin to understanding the theory. These discussions go back, at least, to Aristotle and I don't think it is necessary to go into the finer details here. It might be helpful to differentiate between the two, if it affects how you organise the thinking about and/or delivery of your curriculum. You learn and/or memorise knowledge; you practise skills to get better at them. Therefore, these two branches will lead to different ways of organising pupil progression in the subject.

Deductive knowledge and inductive knowledge

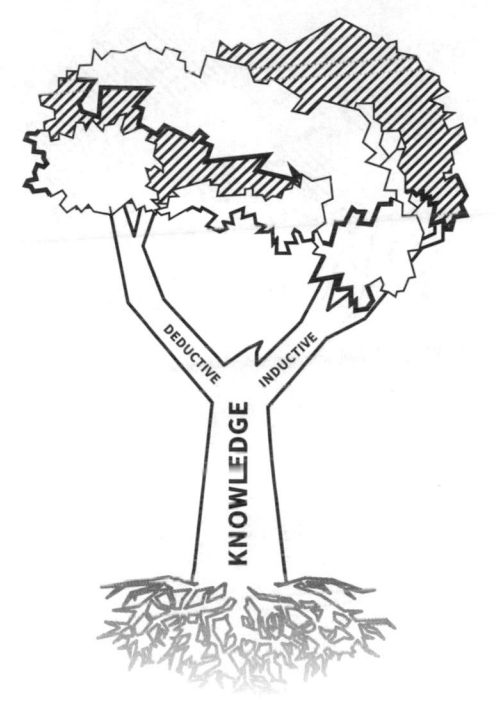

Deductive knowledge is from the general to the specific; inductive knowledge is from the specific to the general. For example, the way one approaches theory might be more 'deductive' in nature, while the practical side of things might be more 'inductive'. This would entail the theory being taught in a more teacher-led way and the practical being more child-centred, in that the child's engagement with the subject is that of an active participant who is learning how to create within the art form with a differing amount of freedom and constraint.

Liberal knowledge and useful knowledge

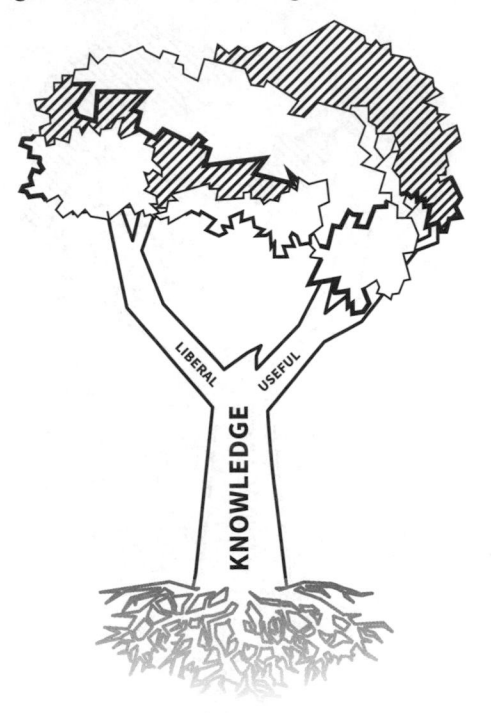

Highly valued classical 'liberal' knowledge dates back to the Greeks. A forerunner of later arguments around 'the best that has been thought and said' and cultural capital, it is the kind of knowledge that might be profoundly useless in a practical sense but is valuable to the exploration of what makes us human. Liberal knowledge is for people with enough leisure time to think about things; for those with a 'love of wisdom' or, as the Greeks put it, *philosophia*, where our word 'philosophy' finds its root.

'Useful' knowledge is what many people suggest our schools should deliver, but schools are, some would argue, noticeably lacking in the ability to teach this stuff. Originally based around the 'mechanical' arts, useful knowledge should now have utility in such things as workplace skills, '21st-century skills', money management, household chores, sex education (arguably), using a spreadsheet…I could go on. Does your curriculum divide into 'vocational and life skills' and 'knowledge for its own sake'?

Art and discipline

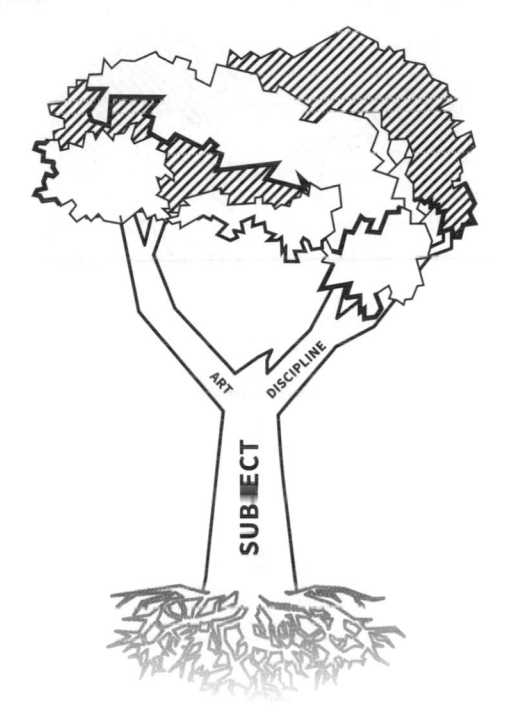

The difference between an art and a discipline is that art seeks to create 'new' knowledge either in a speech, an essay or any other form of new work, whereas a 'discipline' is about replicating knowledge that already exists but might not yet be known by the student. The former is a type of liberal knowledge, usually associated with the medieval trivium: grammar, dialectic and rhetoric. The latter is, clearly, a form of disciplinary knowledge associated with 'useful' knowledge – the sort you might get from an apprenticeship. If you are teaching pupils to be able to think for themselves then the subject is an 'art'. If you wish for them to follow instructions then it is a discipline. Many subjects split between the two approaches and might require organising differently to do both approaches justice.

Memory, reasoning, imagination

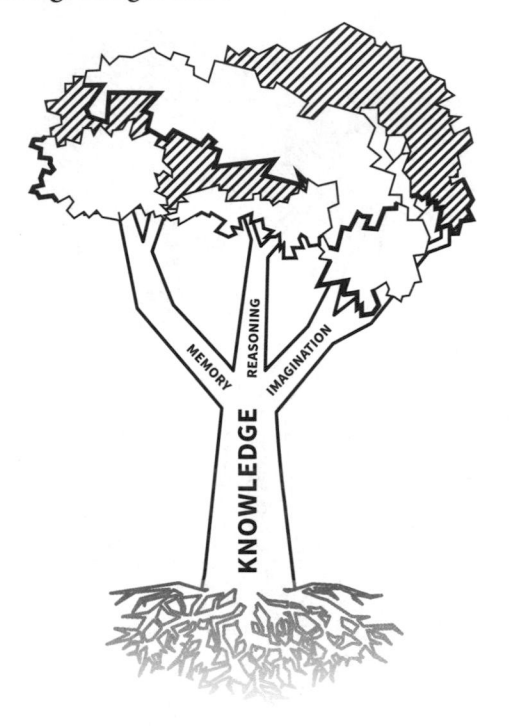

Francis Bacon (1561-1626) divided knowledge into three categories – memory, reasoning, imagination – which had a remarkable affinity with the earlier trivium. Grammar becomes memory, dialectic becomes reasoning, and rhetoric becomes imagination (see also organ, method, illustration). Bacon called his inductive approach to rational knowledge 'the Tradition'. One can easily see where history, philosophy and poetry sat in his curriculum and it might be useful to think of your subject so divided.

Specialised knowledge and general knowledge

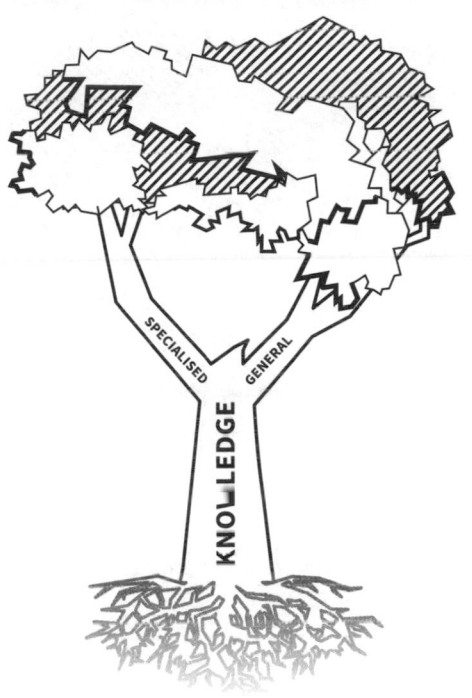

Much of schooling in many countries is about narrowing knowledge into specialisms. Knowing a little about a lot can be a demeaning thing to say about someone, whereas knowing a lot about a specific subject – being an expert – is something usually to be admired. Yet, if we think of this in terms of breadth vs depth, we can begin to see that the two things feed off each other.[8]

---

8   When it comes to what a school is for, I would argue that a general education is a good thing. When specialising in, for example, just three subjects at A level, it would be beneficial for some general, wider education to continue to keep pupils from narrowing too quickly. Recently, I read about a professional footballer who plays for a Premier League team but has found time to study and get good grades in economics and history A levels. I can't help but think that this desire not to narrow his life into 'just football' is a good thing. To know something about everything is difficult with the plethora of information out there, but perhaps a culturally mobile polymath is exactly what we need to be in order to find meaning in this world.

Quantitative knowledge and qualitative knowledge

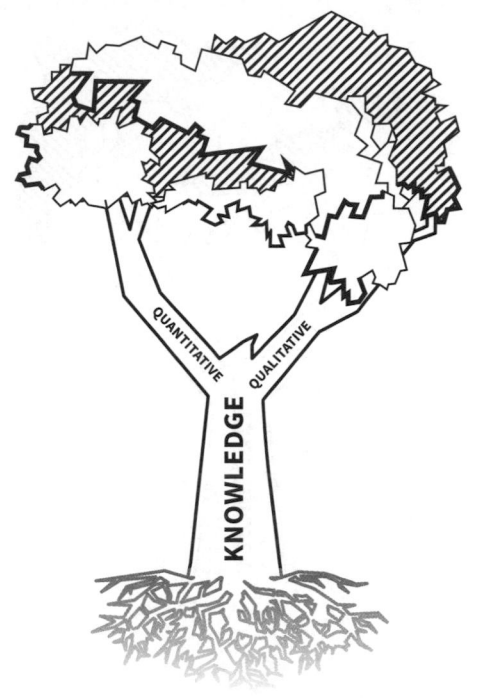

Arguably, quantitative knowledge is increasingly valued over qualitative. Another way to look at it might be 'objective vs subjective knowledge'. Mathematics and various sciences belong more to the former; arts, humanities and some sciences belong more to the latter. These distinctions might be helpful and can impact on such categories as 'substantive' knowledge. In assessment terms, it is easier to gauge progress in the quantitative than the qualitative. Many subjects cover both areas.

Old knowledge and new knowledge

How much of what you are doing when learning is to transmit to memory 'old ideas', and how much is to allow new ideas, thoughts and imaginings to occur? This is the division between rote learning and knowledge creation. The latter might feed off the former, but it is certainly true that schools are not just about transmitting knowledge traditions. We don't just ask pupils to learn poetry by heart; we also ask them to express their feelings and ideas about poems and to write poems of their own. This brings new thoughts and new knowledge into being. New knowledge is not just created by those in the school; new knowledge is accruing in the world all the time. How do we access and/or make use of 'the new'?

Substantive knowledge and disciplinary knowledge

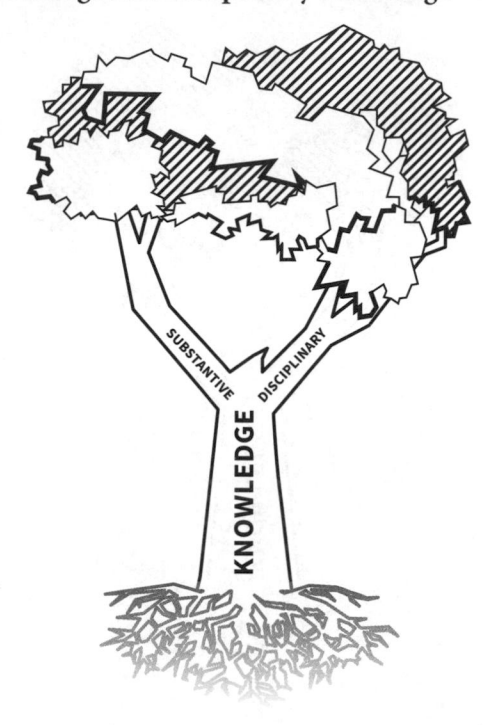

Substantive knowledge is that which is factual – knowledge that is true in a given subject. Disciplinary knowledge is that which helps us to gain the substantive knowledge in a subject.

Knowing how and knowing that

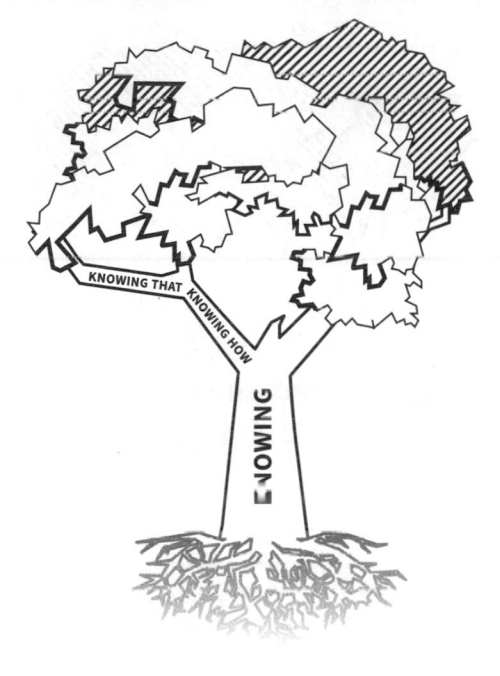

The philosopher Gilbert Ryle's distinction between 'knowing how' and 'knowing that' (ostensibly a distinction between practical and theory) controversially places practical understanding before that of theoretical understanding. We could go down a rabbit hole discussing the order of these things, but suffice it to say that, to Ryle, it is through the use of knowledge that one becomes a master of it. In a traditional, academic environment, know-how is thought of as inferior. Here we can emphasise an alternative order of things: the importance of practice, of doing, of becoming skilful as a way of becoming knowledgeable about theory.

Procedural knowledge and declarative knowledge

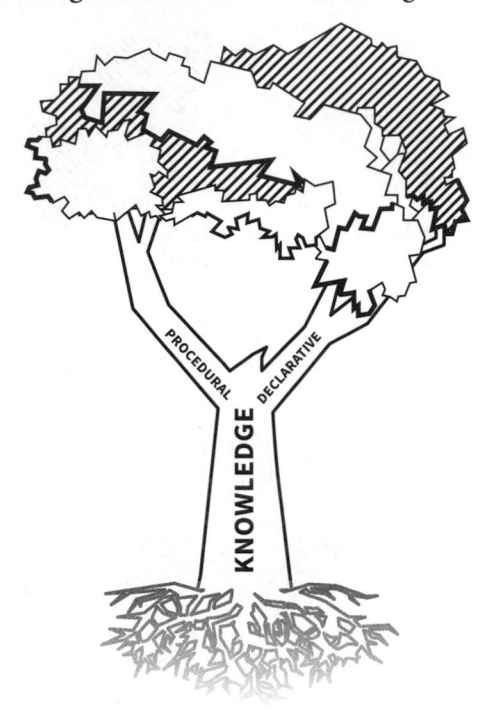

Procedural knowledge is the 'how' rather than the 'what'. It can overlap with disciplinary knowledge and, indeed, 'skills'. It is especially connected to cognitive processes like decision-making, critical thinking, creativity and the like. Declarative knowledge is the 'what'. Similar to substantive knowledge, declarative knowledge is when you know the facts; the truth; that something is the case.

Skills and competencies

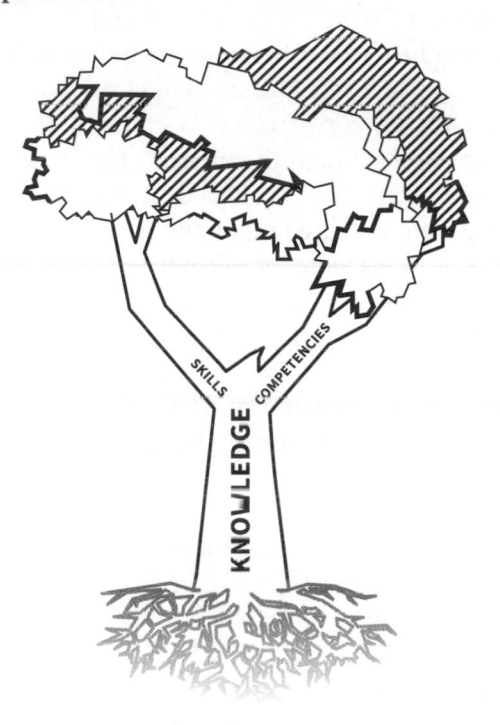

'Skills' seem to be more firmly connected to specific activities, whereas 'competencies' seem to be more general in application. A student might be skilled at playing the violin; they might have the improvisational skills to be able to excel at jazz violin. A student considered to be generally creative might be said to have 'creative competency'. This opens up an issue: 'competencies' point towards an ability to do things across different domains, yet there is a good body of evidence to show that being creative in art does not mean you are creative in mathematics. This is the problem of transferability.

Let's say a pupil is creative in art but not so on a football field. The teacher would have to pick apart and make explicit the aspects of creativity that allow the pupil to excel in art, and show how they could use the relevant parts of the competency on the football pitch. You might think this could be quite laborious for little result – and you might be right.

In fields more akin to each other, you could say that a pupil who has the competency to write an essay in literature class but struggles to write an essay in history could be taught quite easily to transfer this competency across. The history teacher could use the literature essay as a base model, show how a history essay is similar and how it is different, and then take the pupil through the process. The same approach should be used with graphs, statistics, etc. This demonstrates the importance of teachers knowing what is being taught and when in other subjects.

Competencies can become problematic if they aren't specifically relevant to the subject in which they are expected to be featured. This sometimes results in a teacher teaching, say, 'creativity' in mathematics over a Maths Week or Maths Day assessed separately to the rest of the curriculum. These curriculum days might satisfy the need for a competency to be ticked off on a checklist but do little to develop the pupil over time. Some competencies are so difficult to fathom because they are hard to pin down. The Qualifications and Curriculum Authority proscribed a list of competencies for the 2007 English national curriculum that asked schools to teach and assess progress in spiritual, moral, social and cultural development, independent enquiry, creative thinking and effective participation.[9] The problem came when teachers tried to put this into action.

We all *sort of* know what is meant by creativity and culture, for example, but when you begin to explore what these competencies might mean in order to explain them to children, and then assess them fairly so children can understand how they might improve their cultural development, problems occur. One only has to think of what an authoritarian government might suggest these competencies to mean in practice to see how something might go horribly wrong when trying to pin them down precisely.

'Hard skills' and 'soft skills' are another way of describing a similar binary. Hard skills could be considered as more akin to 'skills', while 'soft skills' – those that are more difficult to teach explicitly – could be considered as more akin to 'competencies'.

This area also includes a sense of personal development and progression, some of which is the natural progression of getting older

---

9   https://publications.parliament.uk/pa/cm200708/cmselect/cmchilsch/memo/natcurric/ucm34b02.pdf

and some of which can be shaped partly by what and how you study and who with; the social and cultural mix our pupils are exposed to in school. This 'tacit' curriculum should be thought about and a good framing question is, 'How do we help our pupils to flourish?'

The answers to this question can focus on extracurricular/co-curricular provision as well as curricular, the general atmosphere and ambience of the school, and how 'inclusive' the culture is, as well as how to recognise different strengths and enable children to develop – what is referred to as 'self-actualisation'. Counselling and mental health services may be required when children are struggling. All this matters and supports pupils' individual and collective searches for meaning.

Explicit knowledge and implicit knowledge

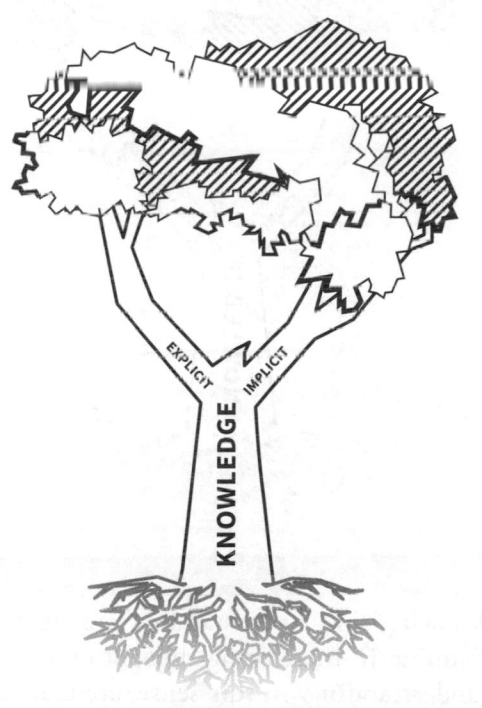

The former is what we know and can tell. The latter is what we know yet cannot tell. These unspoken codes, conventions and ideas that we absorb can be studied and made explicit, and various subjects might excel at this – for example, cultural studies, sociology, anthropology and psychology.

As discussed in chapter 4, we might wish to examine our assumptions and biases when choosing what knowledge to teach. Like the true scientist, the curriculum designer should welcome constructive dissent, but also realise the importance of the implicit knowledge they have absorbed through the culture in which they operate.

Knowing and understanding

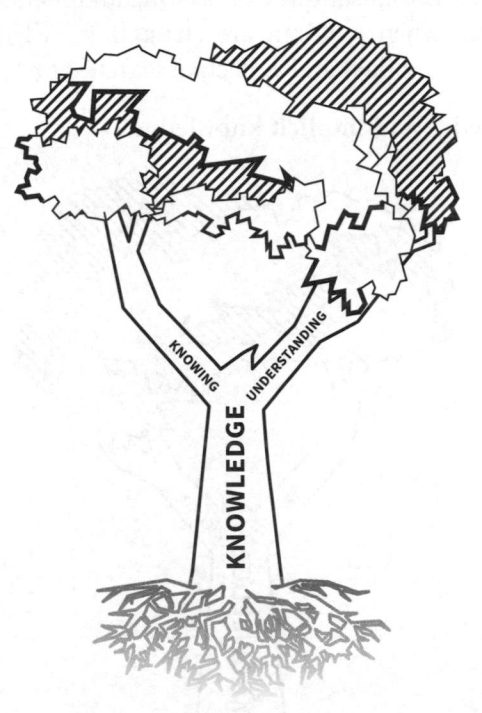

In education, 'knowing' and 'understanding' are often mentioned in the same breath, resulting in their being thought of as one and the same. Knowing and understanding, in this sense, are tautological. For some, 'understanding' can represent depth when we talk about learning. 'Deep learning' is a beloved idea of a good number of educators who try to show there is more to the art of teaching than instilling 'mere' facts to memorise. However, knowledge, as a word, does this on its own, moving us on from the mere learning of facts and information. Yet perhaps 'understanding' goes further towards expertise when it becomes innate and involves an emotional connection. Understanding places the pupil in the midst of something; it exemplifies the idea of belonging.

Maybe we can 'know' something scientifically, but 'understand' something through 'phronesis' – an engagement with the form itself.

The knower, knowing and the known

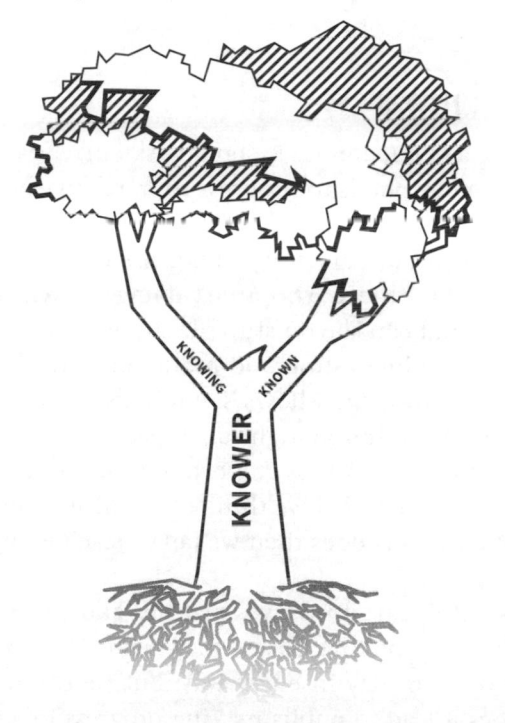

This is the very realisation that things themselves might exist, but with no one to 'know' them, they are not part of knowledge. Objective knowledge in this context is an oxymoron, as all knowledge is known subjectively, by individuals and groups of human beings. It matters *how* this knowledge is known. The quality of knowing something changes both the knower and the known. However, scientific knowledge and 'artistic knowledge' might be known differently, the former relying on the idea of the knower as a disinterested observer. In art, the knower is very much interested – the personal is, arguably, far more important in art than science.

Discussion

- Will branches of knowledge help us to organise our curriculum?
- If so, what branches of knowledge are most useful for our area of focus?

Inner circle: progress

When designing a curriculum, we should ask ourselves, 'What does the process of getting our pupils to progress from relative novices to relative experts look like in this subject?' It might be worth thinking about different pupils who are currently taking the course: those who seem to be coping well and those who aren't doing so well. Does our pupil know about stuff and can she do stuff? Is she able to use her knowledge and skills to produce interesting and profound work that demonstrates a good degree of knowledge, shows she has absorbed it and shows she can use it in interesting and thoughtful/skilled ways? Is she able to carry out subject-specific and similarly important tasks, independently, with a good degree of competence? If we think of a skill as something that only looks like what an expert does then we fail to teach it and just let pupils sink or swim.

Progress is not linear: it involves plateaus and sometimes decline as well as growth. We shouldn't obsess too much about pupils who don't seem to improve every day in every way. But we *can* obsess about our curriculum: does it lead to pupils making progress in a way that builds complexity and expertise? Pupils' skills must develop over time – this is the journey from novice to expert. Of course, by the time they reach a certain age, some pupils will be more expert than others. This does not mean we should treat some pupils as incapable of achieving a good level of success; it does mean we might need to adjust the curriculum to ensure our pupils all achieve a good level of success. A curriculum should not be planned deliberately to fail some pupils.

Curriculum is the progress model

Instead of the onus being on the pupil and their progress, the onus should be on the quality of the curriculum on offer to them. Instead of writing pupils off at a young age or, indeed, them writing themselves off, teachers should take responsibility for how pupils collectively and individually make progress. If there are major problems in their progression, this isn't the fault of 'our kids'. It is the fault of 'our curriculum'.

Teachers need a shared understanding of where pupils are expected to be in terms of knowledge and skills when they leave one class to take up study in another. This expectation is tied to what and how they are taught. Crucial and complex content and skills need time to develop, to sink in, to become a habit. Teachers must know how to build up these more complex understandings and abilities over time as a pupil is taught a concept/idea/how to carry out tasks. For example: the atom; the novel; empires and colonialism; political, philosophical and religious thinking; playing a sport; writing an essay; making an argument; learning to cook, to paint, to dance. All these ideas and fields of study take more than a few weeks to understand fully. They take years. To allow for this, is our curriculum suitably 'growthful'?

Assessment

Each pupil will progress as long as the curriculum progresses. When we stop teaching certain things, pupils' progress also stops. This idea can lend itself to assessment: have they learned what they have been taught? If so, they can be given a percentage mark that relates to the 'amount' of knowledge they have remembered at any one time. But this depends very much on the type of knowledge you are teaching. The more objective the knowledge and the more quantifiable its measurement, the more the curriculum is a good model for the measurement of progression. However, the more subjective and qualitative the curriculum, the less accurate the measurement of progress. This doesn't mean pupils won't progress, because they will, but don't expect any measurement of that progress to be worthwhile when only collected as a set of numbers or letters.

Once your curriculum is in place, it is worthwhile to ask, 'How best to assess the learning that has taken, is taking and will take place?' Certainly, this question should be explored, but don't let it dominate the process. Let the assessment question follow the curriculum by asking, 'How good and how successful is our curriculum and how do we know?'

In order to answer this, we will require some form of assessment:

- The purpose of internal assessment should be twofold. First, it should seek to provide periodic statements of competence stating that students have mastered curriculum content sufficiently well to progress onwards. Second, it should be a mechanism for assuring the quality of the curriculum and how well it is taught.

- Ideally, if the curriculum is perfectly specified and taught, all students would get everything right and be able to do everything perfectly. Clearly, we will never come near this state of perfection, but if we can report generally that there is a very high level of knowledge, skills and performance throughout the student body then we are doing well.

- This approach to assessment is different to traditional, discriminatory assessments in which we try to differentiate between pupils and that can be tracked on a bell curve.

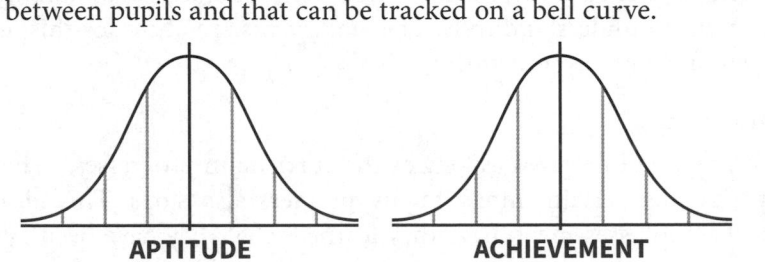

Source: *David Didau*

- An assessment designed to show pupils' mastery of the curriculum should produce something that looks a bit more like a slope.

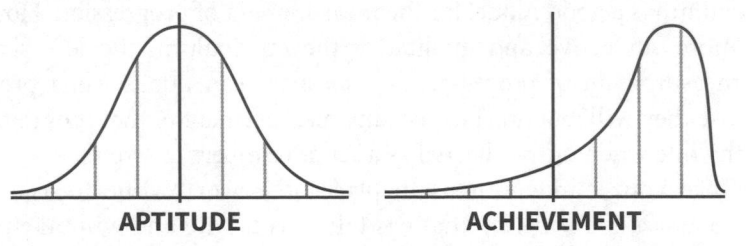

Source: *David Didau*

- A discriminatory assessment is designed to produce winners and losers; to designate some students as 'able' and some as 'less able'. Doing poorly in this style of assessments is likely to create a self-fulfilling prophesy in which students learn early on that they are 'rubbish' at certain (perhaps all) subjects. Whereas, with the emphasis on assessment as a way of examining the quality of the curriculum and teaching, if something doesn't seem to be working we do something about it, both in the short term (by taking responsibility) and in the longer term (by redesign)

- If our guiding assumption is that any poor performance in tests or other forms of assessment highlights some fault in the curriculum or teaching, this could transform the educational experiences of our most disadvantaged students. Instead of seeing tests as demoralising pass/fail cliff edges, they might come to see that they provide useful benchmarks of progress to strive towards.

- In order to ensure our assessments are a fair reflection of our curriculum, we should never assess our students on something that hasn't been explicitly taught.

- Any areas of the curriculum that can be described as 'skills' must be broken down into teachable components of knowledge that can be learned and practised.

- Skills assessments should be broken down into component parts. We shouldn't test a pupil on bike-riding by seeing how they perform in the Tour de France if we have only removed their stabilisers in their most recent lesson.

- If pupils across multiple classes struggle, we should assume the fault is with the curriculum. If pupils in a particular class struggle, the issue is more likely to be with the teaching. If one or two pupils struggle then we need to be critical about how we have made our curriculum accessible to all. In the latter case, it's not always our fault, of course, but one would hope that, with judicious questioning of pupils and keeping in touch with how successfully they are learning the curriculum, any struggles would have been picked up and dealt with earlier.

Not only do we need teaching to be responsive to students' needs, but we also need to think in terms of responsive curriculum. If students struggle with some element of assessment, this is because a 'gap' has been left into which they have fallen.

From content to narrative

This is a vital step. It is where we begin to stop seeing curriculum as a list of one damn thing after another, and start to think of it as a narrative in which new knowledge connects with other pieces of knowledge, and skills and competencies are an intrinsic part of what is being taught. This 'narrative' enables a child to develop in alignment with the subject matter being taught. Rather than fulfilling some esoteric criteria, the curriculum itself enables the pupils to progress. If the curriculum is being learned well, taught well, designed well, then all who study it should be progressing well.

However, once you start thinking about curriculum as narrative, certain problems can occur. This is where the quality of the national curriculum and various textbooks, as well as current and previous curriculum materials and resources, come into sharp relief. Are they any good? Do they fit into our narrative(s)? Are our narratives any good? If in doubt, dump or adapt them, especially if you believe their quality falls short. If you *have* to incorporate them, for whatever reason (legal, financial, political, etc.), can their damaging effect be limited so they can support the quality of the curriculum you are working towards? Perhaps, in the first instance, they can be used as examples to support, guide and point towards potential structures; perhaps they can be used as reference points, as familiar props, as you move onward to better things. If the materials on offer are excellent and fit really well with your needs then embrace them wholeheartedly, but, as always, keep them open to review.

Seeking out what other schools do in terms of content narrative can offer interesting comparisons. Such examples can be found on websites or through your sister schools or other groups. Professional organisations, universities and specialist teachers might be able to provide pointers on what the best content might be and how it might be organised.

It may become apparent that just because the curriculum is written down, this doesn't make it a narrative. Just because a series of things are written along a visual representation – say, a 'curriculum snake' – this doesn't make it a progression model, nor a coherent narrative. One damn thing after another might be 'history' but it sure as hell isn't a good curriculum.

A way of helping to build the narrative is to think about the context of the content. Where does this fit into the wider picture? Have we taught about context? Do our pupils *know* the wider picture? Can they see the wood, or are they looking at too many trees? This all helps to build schemata, which we will consider further in the next chapter.

Discussion

- What are the branches of knowledge we are beginning to build upon?
- Does how we go about teaching the content really impact on the skills and competencies we are trying to engender?
- Thinking about what we are asking pupils to produce and the progress we expect them to make, from novice to something approaching expert, how we go about teaching the curriculum also affects how we might organise it.
- Have we made sure that all our pupils will be able to access this curriculum and be successful?
- Is our curriculum 'growthful'?
- How best to organise the material we need to include in the curriculum?
- Different ways of organising the curriculum content can make a huge difference to how it is taught, how successfully it is understood by the pupils, and how well pupils can develop as independent learners with a suitable level of expertise in a given subject area.

6. Organising and sequencing

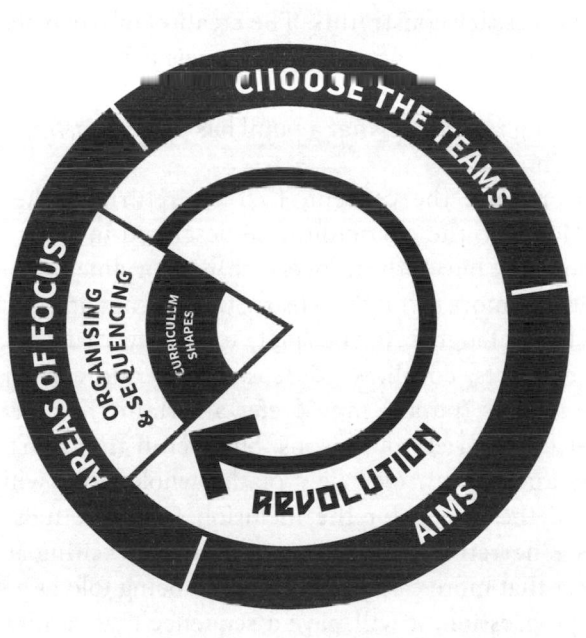

Middle circle: organising and sequencing

This is where curriculum design moves on from just being about lists of content, and begins to be organised and sequenced. A good curriculum doesn't just link sequentially, but also links through mental models – what the psychologist Frederic Bartlett called 'schema'. Schema theory mainly explores how new knowledge has to fit with what is already known in order to be understood. Structuring a curriculum involves layering new knowledge upon older knowledge, and while teachers will seek to make connections with what individuals and groups of pupils already know, they will also link to what they have already taught, therefore connecting not just to the pupils' folk knowledge, the knowledge they have picked up during their lives, but also to their curriculum knowledge.

Central to this is the concept of the mind not being a store of information, but rather being in a dynamic relationship with the environment. Just as a map might help us to navigate a city, a schematic approach to curriculum enables the pupil to navigate the subject, travelling where they want to across the terrain within the limits set by the subject's necessary constraints. The creation of schemata offers tools for navigating a subject, and it allows knowledge somewhere to nestle. These schemata must be based on the underlying structures *as taught*, rather than being reliant on what a pupil has picked up, by chance, inside and outside school.

To help organise the content, first we return to the curriculum 'narrative'. How can the curriculum be described in story form? If the 'story' is a series of bits with no overarching storyline then it will make less sense, will be more difficult to learn and will not help pupils to grasp the subject being taught. As the 'plot' unfolds we will introduce new characters, concepts, conflicts, ideas, artefacts and a myriad of other stories. The readers (pupils) may prefer a certain character or chapter over another for a variety of reasons, but even if they don't take to one character or another, an overview of the whole story will help them to understand the reason for the inclusion. Even the most abstract of subjects has a 'narrative', though it might be less exciting at first glance than a subject that more easily lends itself to being told as a story. It will still have a progression; it will have a sequence that can be shared and understood.

Thinking of the narrative arc of our curriculum helps us make sense of what we are teaching and why; it also helps us to explain to new members of staff or new pupils how what they are teaching or studying might fit into the whole, without having to get bogged down in detail.

Like all the best stories, there are underlying structures that aid us with our curriculum narratives. There is the linear aspect: what follows what, or, in curriculum designer jargon, 'sequence'. An obvious question to ask is, 'What is the best sequence to teach, bearing in mind the increasing maturity of our pupils and the increasing complexity of the topics we are teaching?' Think 'novice to expert'. At this point, it is a useful exercise to get some Post-it notes and a big bit of paper and start putting the content together in possible sequences. Doing so makes clear that 'one damn thing after another' doesn't necessarily help us to tell our subject story or, indeed, stories. Just as some characters and chapters are more important than others, becoming more of a vehicle for the overall understanding of the narrative, so it is with the knowledge and skills we wish our pupils to understand and be able to perform. The 'more important knowledges' are our 'big ideas'.

The big Ideas

If some knowledge is more important than other knowledge for a pupil to learn, is it clear what this knowledge might be? If so, we need to emphasise it somehow. In what way might it be more important?

Some knowledge 'organises' other knowledge – for example, overall concepts, precepts, foundational knowledge, etc. Is it clear what this knowledge might be and how it could be used to navigate the curriculum? From the list of content and information we have begun with, the task is now to fit this together into thoughtful 'webs' of understanding, or schemata. This will start to move your curriculum from a 'one damn thing after another' approach to a more sophisticated and more memorable offer.

It is helpful to think about what 'shape' the curriculum is (T-shaped, upside-down triangles, spirals or Russian dolls for organising principles, or more linear models such as curriculum snakes, blocked topics and curriculum ladders) and how this shape can impact on our thinking (see the next section and chapter 7). In itself, curriculum design has to be simple, but it must also represent quite complex ways of thinking about the world.

If you have models that encourage a linear approach to thinking about curriculum, you might be able to develop skills on a novice-to-expert trajectory, but you are unlikely to be able to unlock 'schematic' curriculum design at a level that really bears fruit. The reason why some pupils find some subjects so difficult is that 'one damn thing after another' leaves individuals to do the hard work of connectivity for themselves.

To demonstrate this, think of something you know about. Now think of all the connections it has to other things (that you know, obviously). This is where it 'sits' in your memory and within the picture(s) you make of the world. Within each subject, things fit together in different ways – and this is what we should be teaching.

Curriculum cohesion is essential. Pupil understanding is based on how well you connect things together in your curriculum, and some ways of connecting things are better than others. When I was 12, my family moved to a different area and I moved to a different school. For whatever reason, I was put into bottom sets for my subjects and then, after a term and a half or so, I was moved into the top sets. However, there was no attempt to teach me anything I had missed by being taught a completely different curriculum in the first school or in the bottom sets as compared with the top sets. I had and still have huge gaps in my knowledge, particularly in subjects like French and maths, and found it difficult to ever truly master them. For me, the dislocated nature of my learning had lasting effects.

Inner circle: curriculum shapes

In curriculum design, we must not just find our way through a syllabus, deliver a script or march through the pages of a textbook. The point of the curriculum revolutions is to join up thinking. Teachers need to have a critical insight into how coherent and joined-up their curriculum is; this means a good amount of time and resources must be given over to collaborative planning, and the revolutions in this book are intended to assist in that process, focusing minds on the task at hand. If schools don't give departments at least an hour a week for co-planning then they are not taking curriculum seriously.

In order to aid cohesive curriculum planning, organisational frameworks can be used to focus the thinking of the curriculum design teams. Can your teachers, separately and together, talk about and evidence not only how their curriculum narrative(s) progress but also how they link to bigger concepts and ideas? Can they map the knowledge and skills, how they intertwine, and how they link to other concepts and ideas that are taught earlier and later? In other words, can they talk about how knowledge is sequenced to help pupils progress in their subject(s), and how the cognitive architecture links together the terrains of knowledge that their subject(s) cover?

This is where curriculum webs and schemata – the underlying architecture of thought – come in. How is the knowledge we teach connected to other knowledge, some of which we might not currently teach? What is the relationship between breadth and depth in the content we teach?

My first job on leaving school was in a university library, where I catalogued books via the Dewey Decimal system. Beloved of librarians and library users, the Dewey Decimal system locates books by their subject.[10] One of the fascinating aspects of the cataloguer's role is trying to decide where a certain book should go, or whether to alter a book's previous place in the system. The Dewey Decimal system can be instructive for curriculum designers. Let's say you want to teach a new topic, a new book or a new piece of knowledge – where should it go? Some might tell you to go straight ahead and teach it, just as some might tell you to put a new book anywhere on a library shelf. Once that book is chucked on the shelf, however, it could get lost and will certainly be more difficult to retrieve. But if it is placed within a defined pecking order, it will be easier to find and a reader might discover some other books around it that are of interest.

If I wanted to locate books on the pre-Socratic philosophers, I would find them in the Dewey Decimal system placed in 182, along from 180 (ancient, medieval and eastern philosophy) in the overall 100 class (philosophy and psychology). Anyone who has catalogued knows that the numbers get more complex as we venture into specifics – and it is this that I want you to think about. If I were seeking a book on the pre-Socratic philosopher Thales, I would go to the philosophy and

---

10   Invented by the controversial Melvil Dewey, the system has outshone its progenitor, who has himself been catalogued as an anti-Semite and sexual predator.

psychology section, look for 'ancient, medieval and eastern philosophy', look for 'Ancient Greeks, pre-Socratics' and there I would find my book. Locating the book involves navigating a knowledge web. It is not linear as such, because many branches are involved.

Now, think of an interesting curriculum paradox. Where would you place Thales in your curriculum? What would come before and what after? Would you teach the pre-Socratic philosophers before you teach Socrates? You could, but you might want to dip into Socrates first in order to locate the pre-Socratics in a 'pre' place. You might already have called your subject 'philosophy', so that has catalogued your part of the web, but would you start with Thales in lesson one? I doubt it. Like the Dewey Decimal system, the broader subjects should come before you dive into the more detailed 'geeky' knowledge.

The idea of using 'curriculum shapes' to help organise your curriculum is explored in some detail in the next chapter. Organising and sequencing your curriculum can be greatly enhanced when you think of the underlying architecture; it is part of the inner wheel as it is a sharp focus on structure that you might not want to get into straight away, but it can help to solve many issues that can undermine some curriculum models. I've put it together as a separate chapter so you can easily navigate to it (or ignore it if you don't see the need for it at this time). One way of deciding whether 'curriculum shapes' might help you can be answering the following questions…

Discussion

- What knowledge connects with other knowledge?
- Do we have major 'knowledge hubs' – big ideas around which other aspects of the curriculum can collect?
- Is our curriculum too messy and disconnected?
- How much clarity do pupils have about the webs we weave together? Does this change over time?
- How well is the curriculum narrative known and shared by all the teachers (and, later, the pupils)?
- Is our curriculum joined up, coherent and sequenced? Is there a connected web (or the beginnings of a connected web)? (*This is explored in the next chapter.*)

- How much do teachers know about what their colleagues are teaching, why and when? Do teachers know this in sufficient detail to refer to, build towards and/or build upon it?
- What shared understanding do we have of how our curriculum might be better joined up?
- What narratives does our curriculum tell about our subject(s)?
- What shape(s), sequences and other organisational frameworks might best be used to organise our curriculum?

7. Curriculum shapes as cognitive architecture

Curriculum shapes help us to build schemata. This 'cognitive architecture' allows us to create curricula that permit webs of connected thoughts and ideas, helping pupils to more easily navigate their way around a subject and more successfully understand what they are learning.

I mentioned a couple of curriculum shapes earlier: a narrow hierarchical structure and a more shallow, wider shape. The former was allied to 'maths', the latter to 'English'. If we drew these shapes they would be similar – rectangles – but the first would be upright and the second lying on its side. What is the shape of your curriculum? It's an interesting question. The shape of a curriculum underpins our 'cognitive architecture' – how we think about the subject. Often this is implicit, rather than made explicit. This chapter is all about how to make the underlying architecture or shape of our curriculum explicit and get it to do what we want it to do.

If we want to build complex structures – ones that allow us to create curricula that enable pupils to master webs of connected thoughts and ideas, helping them to navigate their way more easily around a subject and understand what they are learning in more detail, while also mastering the context – then this chapter shows how this might be done. It also introduces some simple models that can work or can be built upon to allow you to gradually build towards a more complex model.

Cognitive architecture

As Dr Kevin Mitchell, associate professor in developmental neurobiology and genetics at Trinity College Dublin, puts it:

> *All of us gradually build up a web of knowledge … latent schemas that are activated or at least accessible when we detect an example of that type of object or even when we think of it. In this way, percepts are grounded on the basis of stored concepts. And those concepts can get progressively more abstract, encompassing hierarchical categories, causal relations, and narrative sequences of events – all the information that an organism needs, in order to decide what to do in a given situation. The semantic content of a given representation is thus embodied in a web of associations – a set of linkages … the meaning of any current pattern of neural activity is given by the context of stored knowledge.*[11]

The closer we get to organising curricula in a way that enhances our 'web of associations', the better pupils can make sense of the world and, importantly, 'act' in the world – do things that are rooted in understanding. We can call this web of associations our 'cognitive architecture'.

Narratives and hierarchical categories aid understanding – context matters. Other things that help pupils to remember and build their knowledge and understanding include spacing and interleaving. So, if we can design a cohesive curriculum that uses spacing and interleaving to grow a web of knowledge then at least we will be helping pupils to learn, rather than using models that might make it easier for a school bureaucracy to structure a curriculum but do not offer pupils a way to access the *meaning* of their studies.

Interleaving content can be used not just to engineer better recall but also to compare and contrast, to build debates and arguments, and to represent perspectives on big issues and ideas. Hannah Hausman and Nate Kornell suggest that material needs to be related to be effectively interleaved[12] and it is this that informs the examples in this chapter. The

---

11   Mitchell, K. (2022) 'The evolution of meaning – from pragmatic couplings to semantic representations', *Wiring the Brain* (blog), www.wiringthebrain. com/2022/06/the-evolution-of-meaning-from-pragmatic.html

12   Hausman, H. & Kornell, N. (2014) 'Mixing topics while studying does not enhance learning', *Journal of Applied Research in Memory and Cognition*, 3:3

connections made between different things are important if we are to set them up and present them next to each other.

By teaching dialectically, where we look at things from a number of different perspectives, we also better represent the truth about knowledge and culture that is often contested among people who have different ways of viewing the world. This works well in the arts, sciences and humanities, allowing pupils to involve themselves in the cultural complexities of 'knowing' – distinguishing truth from lies, the objective from the subjective, and considering how our changing knowledge about the world might be challenging previous orthodoxies.

By exploring potential curriculum models, we can begin to picture those that provide the best cognitive architecture for the pupil and for the subject being studied. We are moving away from just focusing on instructional design, with its bias towards pedagogy, and on to 'curriculum design', which, of course, also impacts on pedagogy. A well-designed curriculum can support good instructional design, whereas ill-considered curriculum design can stand in the way of good teaching and learning.

In this chapter, we will consider some different curriculum models – curriculum shapes – that can help to build webs of knowledge. First, we will look at a model, used all too often, that provides a chaotic and disconnected curriculum: liquorice allsorts. Next, we will consider a more organised model: blocks. Then two 'linear-narrative' models: snakes and ladders. Then two more complex models that build connectivity, narrative and associations: schemata and webs of knowledge.

Finally, we will look at how to build complexity in a simple way, via a schematic-looking curriculum that allows pupils to grow connections systematically and thoughtfully. We will consider the following curriculum shapes:

- T-shape.
- Upside-down triangle.
- Russian dolls.
- Right-way-up triangle!
- Dialectic/interleaving.
- Spiral curriculum and interleaved/dialectical spirals.

Liquorice allsorts

In the 'liquorice allsorts' model, every teacher can put their hand in whenever they want and take out a few nuggets of knowledge, based on a lesson plan or a scheme of work about a 'topic' or 'theme' that is drawn from the subject but exists as a stand-alone unit of work. This is a surprisingly common approach to curriculum around the world.

A teacher might happen upon a scheme of work, lesson plan or an idea off the top of their head and think, 'Yes, that's a good idea for a lesson (or two)' and then go ahead and teach it, regardless of how it might fit into a wider structure. Whether this conversation takes place in the pub or at a formal staff meeting doesn't mean it will fit well with the overall scheme of things. The resulting lessons might give hints and the pupils might pick up links, but these are often haphazard. The pupils who do best are those who have more existing knowledge by which to judge new knowledge by.

In this model, curriculum is digested in job lots with no consideration of the framing. A pupil might look at different parts of history with no overarching narrative; read a lot of literature but not learn about genres, styles, etc. They might learn about a country here, a geological outcrop there and a river somewhere else, but beyond that have no idea how to navigate the territory. They might look at three paintings, a sculpture, a piece of music and a play or two, but not be able to see beyond them. 'Only connect!' should be our cry. How does our subject tell a grand narrative or narratives? Rather than merely knowing some stuff about some things, pupils need to be able to *navigate* our subjects.

A positive approach to curriculum cohesion can mitigate against this chaos. Teachers working together in teams design a coherent curriculum that makes their job easier and, most importantly, improves their pupils' education. Instead of thinking about topics that represent a 'sample' approach to curriculum design or a linear approach that might work sequentially to tell a straightforward narrative (think history taught chronologically through the kings and queens of England), in this chapter we will explore how certain models of curriculum design can move you towards creating more complex patterns or webs of understanding. Each curriculum revolution will require you to think about which approach might suit you best, bearing in mind that it might take a few revolutions to embed a different model, should you so wish.

Another version of the allsorts model is a heavily child-centred approach that follows the pupil as they make sense of their world. Yes, schemata are formed, but they might not necessarily represent the environment of the subject being studied, if at all. Sometimes arguments are made that this is no bad thing, but you should move beyond this approach into a more structured one. Each of my suggested curriculum models builds up ways to help pupils move around the subject they are being taught. The more sophisticated the models, the better the pupils will be able to navigate the concepts and ideas, locate and understand arguments, place artefacts, people, moments and events and, most of all, make connections that enable them to become more competent and confident in making their own contributions.

Blocks

A blocked curriculum is often used because it makes complete sense on the surface to organise the curriculum tightly around the shape of the school calendar. Each block or topic might last from one holiday period to another. So, there can be up to six topics a year, each with a self-contained scheme of work and set of resources. Each scheme of work might be full of 'activities' that can be used to fill the time or can be dropped in the case of an early Easter. The main point is that these topics fit in with the school year; they are adaptable and changeable, allowing for a good degree of teacher autonomy. The teacher is free to teach topics that interest them, rather than trying to get across the wider thought architecture of the subject being studied.

As part of the curriculum audit (see chapter 10) it might be worth asking children about 'broad' concepts – 'What is a novel?' 'What is modernism?' 'What are particles?' 'What constitutes a continent?' – to see if they can answer confidently and competently. If they can't then a level of understanding of the big ideas is missing. This is likely to be a) reflective of your overall school culture and b) a problem with your curriculum.

Snakes

The next step up from a blocked curriculum is the 'curriculum snake'. At the time of writing, these seem to be ubiquitous. Now, of course, they could be a representation of some quite sophisticated approaches to curriculum design – a timeline. Because the curriculum has to exist in time, one thing *has* to be taught after another.

Curriculum snakes may be useful in providing a visual overview for staff, parents and pupils of what is to come, what has been and where we are on our journey.[13] They can provide an at-a-glance idea of the sequence. This helps to create an impression of progress but, like the blocked curriculum, it can feel like 'one damn thing after another'. The questions to ask about this type of model concern the sophistication of the knowledge and its connections. Does this model construct a web or webs of knowledge, or is it merely a list of topics?

Ladders

From the snake, a step up in sequencing is the ladder. Yes, it's snakes and ladders! If the knowledge is sequenced really well then the growth of knowledge from novice to expert can take place. From simplicity to complexity; from one subject opening 'a door' to the next. When a new topic is introduced, the teacher can go all the way down the ladder and climb the connections back up. Although this may help to alleviate some of the problems with linear models, a curriculum ladder still has the limitations of all linear models.

Schemata

We can understand a schema as a cognitive web by which we organise and think about information that exists 'collectively' outside the mind – it is how we organise the content that we teach. The schemata that already exist within pupils' minds will connect with the subject we teach,

---

13   Although not only are curriculum snakes typically laid out from bottom to top, making them counterintuitive to read, but they are also often festooned with unhelpful 'decoration' in the form of meaningless icons provided owing to a partial understanding of dual coding theory.

and pupils will reach an understanding of what we teach. Although schemata can be positive and negative, true and untrue, helpful and unhelpful, we want to focus on the former, in each case, to ensure our pupils do not begin to hold misconceptions that build up over time and are difficult to unpick.

Just as, internally, we make sense of new information by referring it, organically, to our existing schemata – rejecting it if it does not easily fit in – in our curriculum schema we can make sense of new information by showing how it connects to our external subject schemata. 'This is the whole web we are creating for you – and this little bit fits here.'

I have seen teachers draw connective 'webs' where the topics taught are linked across subjects. For example, a piece of string and two drawing pins on a 'curriculum wall map' link George Orwell's *Animal Farm* when it is taught in literature to the Russian Revolution when it is taught in history. That the vast majority of pupils in the school would read *Animal Farm* but only a minority studied the Russian Revolution didn't seem to matter. But it does. If the connection matters enough then it needs to be taught. We can't rely on the teacher saying, 'Oh, this is about the Russian Revolution – look, here's Trotsky' if a good number of children are distanced from the 'secret' codes that some of their classmates have at their schema-tips.

The teacher's job in the classroom is to open up new information to people who might not always be receptive. (How do we link subject-specific schemata to our pupils' schemata?) The curriculum designer's job is to ensure that where these connections are vital within a subject, they are made explicit.

Discussion

- People organise concepts into mental constructs/schemata. How well do we replicate this in our curriculum shape?
- Schemata help people to process and remember information. Can we recreate these chains of thought?
- New information that fits into existing schemata is more easily understood and therefore recalled. Are we allowing new information to fit into our shared schemata?
- Information that doesn't fit into an existing schema can be easily forgotten. Can we check for understanding, not just about

new knowledge but also about where it fits and connects in the great scheme of things?

What follows over the next few pages are some ideas for how to construct your curriculum schemata simply, while enabling quite 'complex' cognitive architecture to be formed.

Webs of knowledge

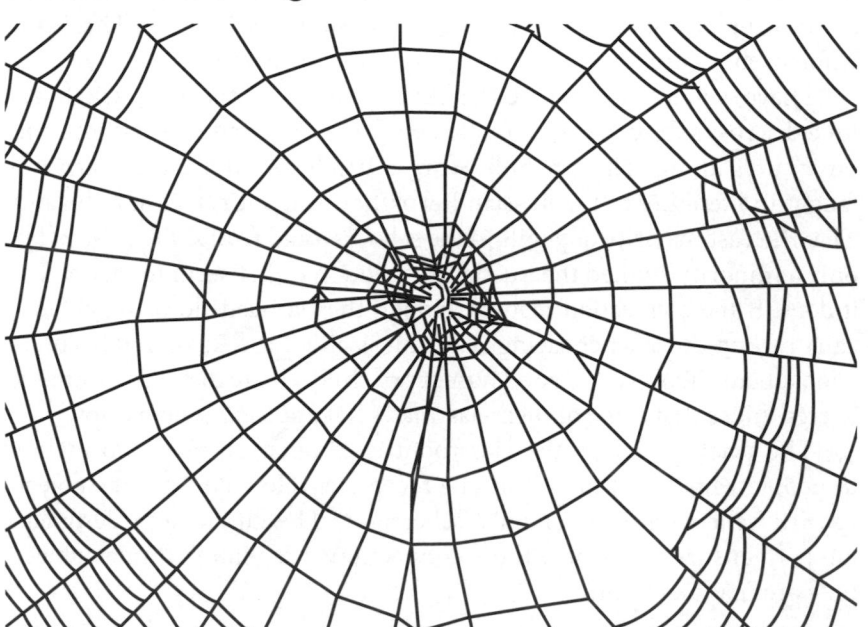

A problem that arises for the curriculum designer is that there are so many potential connections that can be made. A useful exercise is to think about the connectivity within the subject as it is taught now – what links to what – and then consider how much of this is taught, served by the cognitive architecture of your current curriculum. What matters here is not what the teachers think; the real strength of the knowledge web, the connections that your curriculum makes, can be ascertained by asking pupils individually about the connections they have been taught.

So, what to do? First, we can begin to ask hierarchical questions. What bits of knowledge 'organise' other bits of knowledge? ('Particles' might be an organising idea, as might 'novels' or 'empires and colonialism'.) What does the knowledge we are teaching require in terms of previous learning? What are we taking for granted that pupils might know? How do we know they possess this knowledge? Where does our curriculum point to future learning? Are there any connections to be made across the curriculum? These questions could be knowledge- and/or skills-based.

There are so many connections that can be made that the whole thing can end up being completely chaotic. So, to build complexity in a simple way – via a schematic-looking curriculum that allows pupils to grow connections systematically and thoughtfully – I recommend the following shapes:

- T-shape.
- Upside-down triangle.
- Russian dolls.
- Right-way-up triangle!
- Dialectic/interleaving.
- Spiral curriculum and interleaved/dialectical spirals.

T-shape

Instead of a linear model, where one thing follows another, the T-shaped curriculum can be thought of as developing a relationship between depth and breadth. In many linear models, people talk about teaching fewer things in greater depth. This is a mistake. In order for children to be able to traverse the terrain of a subject on their own (which must be an ultimate aim of any curriculum worth its salt) they need to understand the broad brushstrokes that are a way into understanding a subject. A world map might not help you when you're on a foreign holiday and looking for the nearest bank, but does it teach you about the country you are in, its relationship to the country you came from, and its relationships to other countries and continents? Some even feature pictures of other planets and the solar system.

In other words, context reveals a lot about the venture you are about to undertake. The T-shaped curriculum helps us to formulate the broad contextual brushstrokes we should be teaching and how we can exemplify those in terms of where and when to go deeper. The T-shape is understood, quite simply, in this way: the horizontal line of the T represents breadth while the vertical represents depth.

Without overcomplicating it, and instead sticking to the competing notions of breadth and depth, this concept can be useful when thinking about curriculum design. In his book *A Short History of Europe*, Simon Jenkins, somewhat of a contrarian, writes:

> *I disagree with syllabuses that maintain history is better taught in depth than breadth. Depth should follow breadth, for without it history is meaningless. Without awareness of the timeline of human activity, individuals become dissociated figures on a bare stage. Those who cannot speak history to each other have nothing meaningful to say. Context – which means a sense of proportion – is everything.[14]*

And on this matter, he is correct. A knowledge-based curriculum could easily become a list of facts. But if a *knowledge-rich* curriculum is sought then it will be enriched by knowing the context in which the items of knowledge sit. This context can be extremely broad and, yes, it can cross subject boundaries (think of the context of modernism or the

---

14   Jenkins, S. (2018) *A Short History of Europe: from Pericles to Putin*, Viking

Renaissance, for example). It can be concept-oriented or values-driven. Without the breadth, depth can be left bereft.

What balance is needed between depth and breadth? The answer is context-dependent. Some subjects cover less terrain than others; some require such a range of content it is difficult to see how to make time and space to cover much wider breadth at all. In other words, sometimes you are in danger of not seeing the wood for the trees, or not seeing the trees for the wood. The complexity of some subjects means that teachers continually struggle to get the balance right. The following shape is intended to help – a more nuanced approach to the balance between depth and breadth.

Upside-down triangle

It can be helpful to think of the T-shape as an 'upside-down' triangle.[15] This model allows us to consider how knowledge is partly/wholly contained in other knowledge. This 'deductive' approach can be contrasted with the right-way-up triangle, or 'inductive' approach.

The upside-down triangle corresponds to the T-shaped curriculum, where the horizontal line represents breadth and the vertical equals depth. The triangle, however, is more 'graded', in that it gives you a way of getting to the point and, indeed, a point to get to.

Let's look at the example on the next page. Instead of just teaching the song *R.E.S.P.E.C.T.* and then moving on to another piece of music, a more connected curriculum can use context not just to quickly contextualise, in this case, a particular song, but also to teach a good amount of knowledge that connects the song to style, genre, history, etc. Preloading contextual information helps to build knowledge of the song itself and to establish possibilities for future connections to be made as we build our musical schemata. For example, 'soul music' can be referred to when associated genres are explored, like jazz, R&B, its roots in gospel, other soul artists and particular songs. We could explore, of course, the

---

15   I know, it's not really an upside-down triangle, but if you ask most people to draw an upside-down triangle this is what they produce. The 'top' of the triangle (the wider bit) is context and the 'point' is detail. The top is breadth and the journey to the point gives us depth.

particular structure of the song itself and relate that to other forms of 'popular music'. I'm not telling you what to include in a triangle – this is a simple model and there can be many more than just three layers. But notice how a sequence of knowledge is being formed here, logically, from a 'bigger idea' through a 'hierarchy' of contexts: first soul music, then Aretha Franklin, then the song itself.

This means that context is not just one thing. Think of Mary Shelley's novel *Frankenstein*: what is its context? It's a novel, for a start: what is a novel? It's a Gothic novel: what is the Gothic? To understand the Gothic, maybe an understanding of Romanticism is in order, and to understand Romanticism, maybe an idea of the Enlightenment is necessary. Each of these gives a context in which *Frankenstein* could sit. When Charlotte Brontë's *Jane Eyre* is introduced, it too can be placed in the Gothic tradition – a tradition that students will already understand as they have met it before, in the case of *Frankenstein*.

So, T-shape or upside-down triangle – take your pick. The latter gives you a richer web of knowledge.[16]

---

16   This model also turns out to be helpful in exam-answer structure for essays and paragraphs – things are placed in context. When teaching children to write, if they have a structure already in their thought architecture it is easily adapted.

Russian dolls

| VEHICLES | CARS | SPORTS CARS | BRITISH SPORTS CARS | BRITISH SPORTS CARS 1960s-70s | MG |

Another way of thinking about the 'upside-down triangle' curriculum shape is Russian dolls. We could spend a lot of time teaching about the littlest doll without considering what contains that doll, and that doll, and that doll. Each item of knowledge in the curriculum is contained within/catalogued by/organised by some other knowledge. Knowledge is contained in other knowledge: from breadth to detailed depth. What are the bigger ideas that contain the smaller ones? Teach context, to help build connections, so that when something new is learned it already has somewhere to place itself.

Tessellation of upside-down triangles

As you can see, 'upside-down triangles' can be put together to form a 'web' of associations.

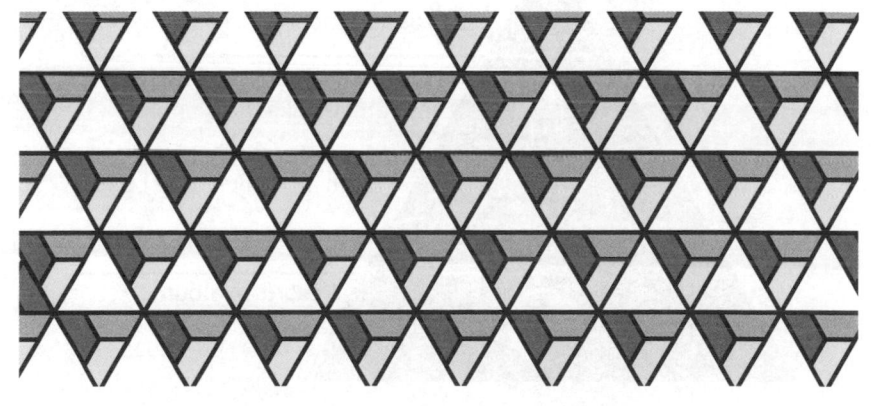

95

Think of one of these triangles as the previously discussed *Frankenstein* triangle. The 'point' (*Frankenstein*) points to the start of two other triangles; maybe one of these could be 'science fiction' and the other 'horror'. It's really up to you. It could be that *Frankenstein* points to the study of *Frankenstein* in more depth (one would hope so). The point is that you can begin to make connections by thinking about how things link without making crazy connections all over the place. Connections can arise from carefully constructed sequences of learning and the interplay between breadth, depth and hierarchies of knowledge.

Right-way-up triangle

The inductive approach, where we start with something small and build up to something big, can be represented through the 'right-way-up triangle' (I know…). This approach works, unsurprisingly, in the opposite way to the other-way-up triangle! Perhaps we begin our foray into learning music practically, by finding middle-C on a keyboard; we might end it by performing a farewell stadium tour with our band and an orchestra. The approach for practical learning often takes this form. That we might learn about the theory and history side of music through the deductive approach shows that there can be a schism between the different approaches to the curriculum within one subject (this is where the knowledge trees can help us).

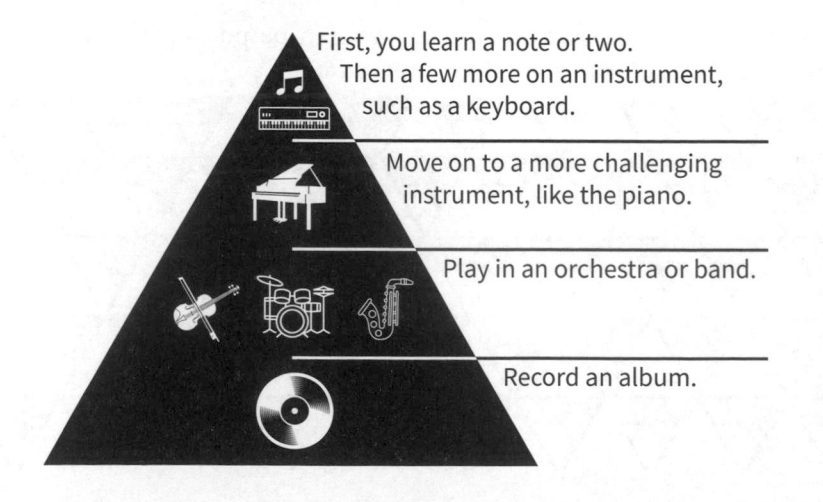

First, you learn a note or two. Then a few more on an instrument, such as a keyboard.

Move on to a more challenging instrument, like the piano.

Play in an orchestra or band.

Record an album.

It is possible to imagine the relationship between the two triangles side by side: the deductive one organising 'theory' and the inductive one organising 'practical'. In an art class, Michelangelo's *David* might come before Carl Andre's pile of bricks in the theory part of the class, but in practical it's a lot easier to do them in the opposite order (with a lot in between). This is one example of why teaching all things chronologically doesn't necessarily work. If you look back at the tessellation you can see how the triangles nestle together but follow different structures from the general to the particular and from the particular to the general. I'm not sure it will always be neat and making connections across is not always obvious, which is why, sometimes, it is important to make the connections explicit, even by exploring differences and conflicts where they occur.

Dialectic/interleaving

Imagine putting a Monet painting next to a Van Gogh. Side by side they explain more of themselves – what they are and are not – than they do if you only see one or the other. When designing a curriculum, we can look for deliberate examples to teach separately and then bring them together to compare, contrast and create discussion and argument as to the relative qualities of each. In a politics class, instead of just teaching, say, Conservatism, or doing a term on Conservatism and a term on Liberalism and a term on Socialism, we can look at them separately, yes, but we can also look at them in comparison with each other. Students learn more and understand more through this dialectical approach.

In my theatre class I would interleave and create dialectic between realism and anti-realism, between 'true-looking representations' and abstract representations that told, maybe, 'deeper' truths. The course became structured around these debates, focusing on truth and its representation. The spiral model can help us to do this successfully...

Spiral curriculum

In his book *The Process of Education*, Jerome Bruner writes:

> *A curriculum as it develops should revisit ... basic ideas repeatedly, building upon them until the student has grasped the full formal apparatus that goes with them.*[17]

This idea is central to the spiral curriculum. In every subject there are ideas, concepts and foundational knowledge upon which the subject is built. Some of these might be argued about, and should be, but the point is to ascertain the organising principles around which a subject curriculum might flow. These 'basic ideas' recur. This is how spacing can be factored into the curriculum: you space the study of the big ideas and revisit them with increasing complexity over time, illustrating the ideas with different examples. The study spirals around, returning to the big ideas and thus strengthening schemata, building rich webs of broad knowledge, and allowing pupils to position deeper knowledge within the wider picture. Instead of 'one damn thing after another', with no connection, we put the foundations in place for new knowledge, as it arrives, allowing for a rich educative experience that can serve children for the rest of their lives.

If we think about painting in an art curriculum, we know it covers a lot of different techniques, tools, paints, styles, eras, artists, etc. Each

---

17   Bruner, J.S. (1960) *The Process of Education*, Harvard University Press

time we revisit 'painting', we learn more about painting as a whole, as well as the particularities being taught at the time. It would be ridiculous to teach painting all at once and never return to it. By returning later, the learning is reinforced.

We can think about forgetting as a way to forge better learning. 'Forgetting' can be seen as simply a difficulty in accessing knowledge, so the attempt to re-find it can enhance its 'retrieval strength'. By revisiting previously learned knowledge we can give pupils a context in which they have to remember what went before. Diligent questioning aids this process.

This is a lot different to the blocked curriculum, where something is taught and then completely forgotten as the learning has moved on to completely different topics. It seems sensible to keep returning to and building upon what has been taught before, rather than leaving it alone once taught. 'We do painting in the autumn term of Year 7' doesn't really cut it. This 'spacing' effect and the increasing interval between 'study opportunities' is a well-researched area. In an article, the cognitive researchers Robert and Elizabeth Bjork write:

> *Perhaps the ultimate example of a manipulation of the conditions of study or practice that produces forgetting, but enhances learning, is the 'spacing effect.' As we have all experienced, when the recall of some studied material is tested after a delay, the longer the delay, the poorer our ability to recall that material, that is, the more we forget. If, however, the material is restudied after a delay, rather than tested, increasing the delay between such study episodes has benefits, not costs, in terms of one's ability to recall the material at a later time, and substantial benefits.[18]*

By spiralling around, we return, but when we return we build upon previous knowledge and thus expand the pupils' repertoire. This is where 'big ideas' – organising concepts – can help us. I worked with a junior school that was teaching 'the Egyptians' one year, 'the Romans' another year, 'the Aztecs' and 'the Victorians' in further years. Rather than dismantle this sequence, we looked at how to make it work by searching for context beyond the subject 'humanities', which was where it sat in the

---

18   Bjork, R.A. & Bjork, E.L. (2019) 'Forgetting as the friend of learning: implications for teaching and self-regulated learning', *Advances in Physiology Education*, 43:2, 164-167

curriculum plan. We decided upon 'civilisations' and looked for unifying threads that we could explore in all cases.

Interleaved/dialectical spirals

The big organising ideas can spiral around each other, revisiting and building upon previous concepts and ideas, as well as reaching across and creating a dialogue with other organising ideas. Realism can contrast with more abstract work. Nature with nurture. 'Leadership and power' can argue with 'insurgents and revolutions'. Empires with colonialism. Think about how a spiral can interact with another spiral. We could be teaching art: in one spiral we are looking at realism and in another spiral we could be looking at abstract and conceptual art. Music could look at classical and popular. Politics: Conservatism and Liberalism. Science: natural science and the social sciences.

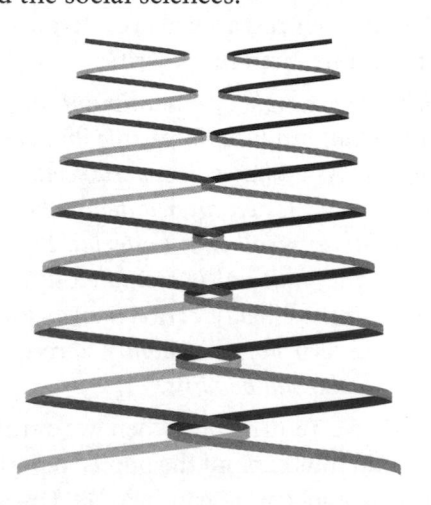

These ideas can spiral separately but they might come together at points – see the interleaving spirals above. Art, science and humanities can be compared and contrasted, tested against each other. Two novels might be studied separately at first and then brought together in some lessons. This way, the pupils learn more about both than they ever would by experiencing them in silos.

Discussion

- What are the organising principles, ideas, concepts, precepts and foundational knowledge in the subject you teach? A knowledge-rich curriculum can be built around these, ensuring good retention, good thinking, 'joined-upness', good progress and a curriculum in which the central narrative(s) and tenets are clear.
- How best to organise the knowledge you wish to teach with these big ideas?
- What curriculum shapes will help you to deliver a curriculum that enhances pupils' understanding of your subject?
- Do we teach the context in a way that enables understanding?
- Is the schema we are teaching sensitive to pupils' differing schemata and to different cultural and social perspectives where relevant?

8. How best to teach it?

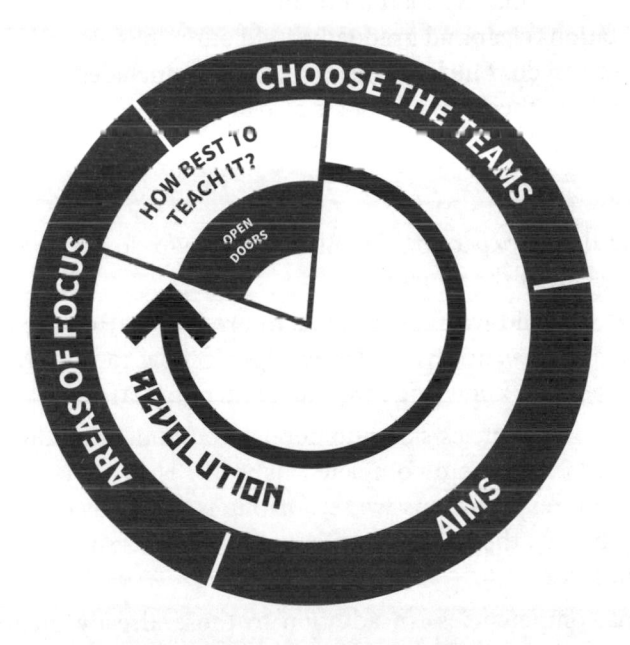

Middle circle: how best to teach it?

Much of the work of our revolutions so far has been on how pupils progress through the curriculum. But now it is useful to consider how teaching might best *encompass* the curriculum. In other words, we have looked at the 'what', the 'when' and the 'why', and now is the time to revisit the 'how'. We can ask not only how pupils' knowledge progresses over time, but also what they can *do*. We can start exploring the integration of skills development, competencies and content. The pedagogy that we use to teach the curriculum changes how it is experienced by the pupils. This is why curriculum designers often emphasise the difference between the 'intended' curriculum and the 'enacted' curriculum; while the former might be languishing on a website, the latter is what takes place in the classroom.

This is the 'practical' curriculum. Practical in the sense of how teachers teach, but also practical in the sense of how the pupil develops their ability 'to do'. This might be making a pot, drawing a picture, setting up an experiment, translating a passage, writing a story or an essay, performing in a play, captaining the football team. Whatever it is, we need to make our expectations clear and gradually build our pupils' competencies/skills so that they *can* do. Much of this expectation is included in how we build our curriculum, theoretically, but is also affected hugely by how we build our curriculum delivery in the classroom.

Discussion

- What do we expect our pupils to be able to do, independently, by the end of the course?

- What work do we expect pupils to produce during the course? How do we ensure their knowledge of 'how to do' progresses alongside the knowledge we expect them to learn?

- What competencies/skills do pupils need to develop during the course to help them complete this work? How do we grow the tasks and expectations we set for pupils, in terms of any skills and abilities they need to have in our subject, so they are able to succeed?

- What competencies (in addition to those already mentioned) are we being asked to teach explicitly during the course (these usually come from outside the subject area and might reflect school or government expectations, such as 'Our pupils are encouraged to be independent learners'). Is this subject suitable for developing these skills?

- How do we best enable pupils to develop these competencies/skills?

- Thinking about the progress of pupils from relative novices to relative experts, how best can we develop their subject-specific skills and abilities, as well as their understanding of the content? For example, classroom discussion – how do we teach children how discussion and debate work in the classroom? And how do we develop this over time so that we start small and build up the complexity over the months and years?

- It might be worthwhile to explore the ramifications of this quote from the philosopher Julian Baggini: '..."transferable critical skills" turn out not to transfer so well after all. Styles of thinking that work brilliantly in some domains fail miserably in others: indeed, some of our biggest mistakes arise when we transfer a way of thinking apt for one domain to another where it just doesn't fit.'[19]

- How can we judge the success of the teaching of competencies and skills?

- How can we judge how pupils are developing as mature learners, becoming more adept in each subject area?

- How do we know if the teaching of competencies and skills is merely a tick-box exercise, or is an embedded and necessary part of the curriculum that improves the quality of knowledge acquisition and scholarship?

Inner circle: open doors

This aspect of the revolution is about ensuring a culture of sharing. The 'open door' policy recognises that although teachers can talk about what they do, it can be better to actually communicate this through 'doing and viewing', or even sharing the teaching at any particular time. Stop just relying on explanation in meetings about what to do and start *showing* and sharing what you do with each other. Then discuss with your colleagues in a mutually supportive way how the challenges and

---

19   Baggini, J. (2021) 'The Hume paradox: how great philosophy leads to dismal politics', *Prospect*, www.prospectmagazine.co.uk/philosophy/david-hume-paradox-philosophy-politics-mistakes

the opportunities of the curriculum are presenting themselves. Seek to answer the following questions through observation and teaching alongside each of your colleagues.

Discussion

- Skills and competencies must be matched with the right subjects and developed alongside growing pupils' independence. Is this a suitable subject? Is this a suitable time for 'group work'? Are our pupils prepared for a good standard of debate and argument at this point in their studies? If not, what do we need to change earlier?

- Do all teachers understand the process involved in teaching skills and competencies alongside knowledge acquisition? Are pupils ready for doing/studying the subject at this level?

- Are any teachers/subjects relying on 'one-off' or separate activities to deliver evidence on how pupils are developing their skills and competencies?

- Do we anticipate any resistance to potential changes to the curriculum and its delivery in light of the explicit teaching/ developing of particular competencies and/or skills?

- How can we ensure our curriculum conversations focus not just on knowledge acquisition, but also on the growth, over time, of suitable skills and competencies that enable pupils to develop successful habits as practitioners in each discipline? Can we make sure the conversations represent what is actually happening?

- How do practical and theoretical knowledge sit side by side in a suitable and successful way?

- What have we learned from each other and how can we ensure others learn from this? Remember, this is best communicated by doing and discussing, rather than focusing on theory alone.

9. How well is it being understood?

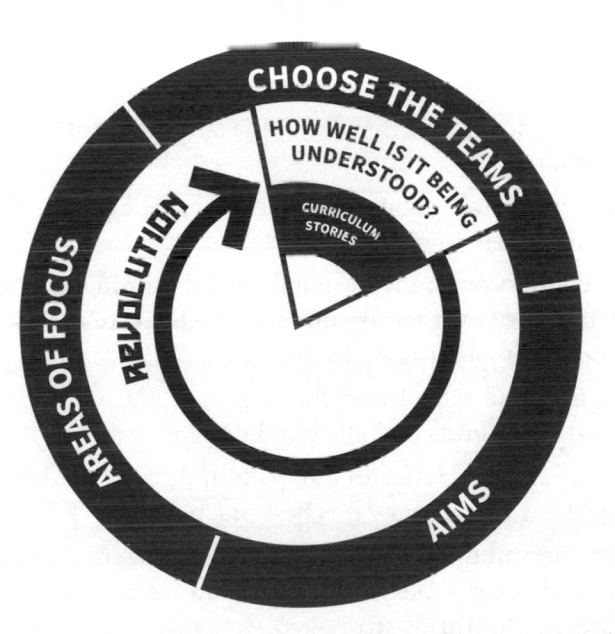

One of the ways to establish the quality of our curriculum is to ascertain how well the pupils understand what they are being taught. One of the ways to do this is to collect and audit assessment data, with the usual caveats about the quality of the data. Another way is to check understanding, periodically, through relevant testing and regular questioning. This way, subject teachers get a good impression of how well the learning has landed. Non-subject experts can look at the accrued data and make general assumptions about how well teaching and learning is progressing. However, there are questions that a non-expert can ask pupils and teachers to help build up an idea of how coherent and cohesive the curriculum is. The expectation would be that these type of questions reveal fascinating information about how the curriculum is being understood by a range of stakeholders.

This could be a good role for the 'critical friend', as they can then feedback what they have learned during the audit process.

Middle circle: how well is the curriculum being understood?

- How well are pupils learning about the subject and how do we know?
- Do pupils know where they are in the curriculum story and how do we know?
- Can the pupils talk about the broad concepts/big ideas that help to organise their studies in a subject?
- What connections can the pupils make within their areas of study to show how they are building a schema of the subject?
- How do we know how well the curriculum is being learned throughout the school and the impact it is having on pupils' knowledge, progress and all-round development?
- What does best practice in curriculum design look like in our school? How do we know it is best practice?
- Is our curriculum coherent? Does it make sense to teachers, pupils and other stakeholders? How do we ascertain whether the evidence for this is strong?
- How well can pupils explain what they have learned, what they know about and what they can now do better than they could before?

Inner circle: curriculum stories

This process is to test whether the curriculum is coherent and whether its organisation makes sense to pupils. It cultivates ongoing pupil/teacher dialogue and broadens the scope of curriculum conversations by looking at how well the curriculum aims are being achieved.

- How well can pupils explain what they are learning now, what they are beginning to understand and what they are beginning to be able to do?

- How well can pupils explain what they are yet to learn, what they do not yet understand and what they are not (yet) able to do?

- Do these narratives match up to their teachers' curriculum understanding?

- Is there a shared understanding of the curriculum narratives between teachers and pupils?

- Depending on the outcomes of the curriculum conversations between teachers and pupils, what lessons can be drawn about the coherence of the curriculum?

- If pupils are not able to share in an understanding of the curriculum narratives, where does the fault lie?

If problems are uncovered then questions could be asked about whether the issues are to do with curriculum content and connectivity, the overall curriculum design, the quality of teaching and learning, or a failure of communication. The principal and curriculum leaders can think of questions to ask all members of the team to ascertain the consistency of curriculum thinking and teaching.

10. Audit and review

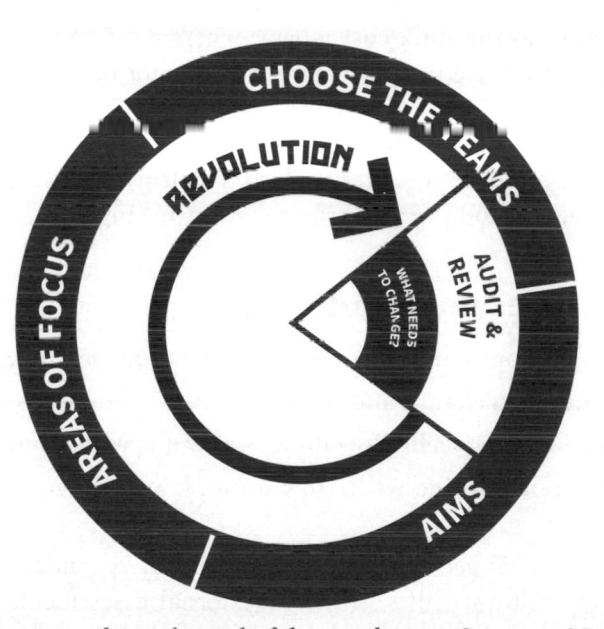

We are now approaching the end of the revolution. Or are we? I wasn't sure where to place this chapter, for it is as much an end as it is a beginning. In fact, if this is your first revolution, I would highly recommend beginning here. ('Now he tells us!' I hear you scream.)

The audit is essential. You might find out that your curriculum ain't broke and doesn't need fixing. But then, you might uncover small areas that need tweaking or, indeed, the need for major surgery. What follows are some questions to ask at different levels of your education establishment. You might wish to adapt, add and/or take away some of the questions below – after all, you know your circumstances better than anyone else and will be able to focus your questioning accordingly.

The important thing is to retain an air of critical detachment. If you have appointed a critical friend, this might be a good task for them to carry out. If we have invested a lot in our curriculum, it might be that we wish to defend it or build upon what we have done, even if it is clear to some that it is not working. This is the time to be less defensive of what has passed and more critical of it. Making changes now for the future is what matters, rather than trying to carry on with something that is no longer useful to us, just because we have 'always done it' or we 'quite like it'. This is akin to the sunk cost fallacy, where we continue with things as they are because we have already invested a lot of time, energy and/ or resources.

Your critical detachment is vital, whether this is your first or fourth or fortieth revolution. Be prepared to challenge and change where necessary, but also to keep and grow what is working.

Middle circle: audit and review

- How well is our curriculum working? How do we know?
- What needs to change and why?
- What is working well? How do we know it is working well?
- What is not working well? How do we know it is not working well?
- What has changed (externally or internally or, indeed, a mix of both: cultural shifts, shifts in external assessments, policy shifts to subjects and/or what is being studied, etc.) to make certain areas of the curriculum no longer helpful to our overall curriculum narrative?
- How well are pupils responding to the curriculum? How do we know?
- How well are pupils understanding what we are teaching? How do we know?

- Are pupils becoming more independent, more knowledgeable and more skilful? How do we know?
- Evidence the quality of output from pupils at different points during their studies. How secure are our judgements?
- How do we know this is the right content for our pupils to learn?
- How do we collect evidence? Is it relevant and adequate?
- How do we know that our teachers' knowledge is sufficient to teach this content well?
- How well do our teachers understand the curriculum and how it all connects?
- Do we need to do more to improve the shared understanding of how the curriculum connects?
- Is the curriculum content successfully understood by pupils?

Inner circle: what needs to change?

- What ought to be changed?
- What are the areas of concern?
- What regular issues continue to crop up around pupil misconceptions?
- What are the real strengths and successes of the curriculum?
- Audit the quality of curriculum content. Question 'Why this and not this?'
- Are the same curriculum narratives shared by all?
- What might be our professional development requirements?

  – Subject knowledge: do staff need training in any new content and how it fits into the overall curriculum?

  – Do staff require training in pedagogical approaches to teaching the curriculum?

  – What training might be required?

  – How do we ensure this training is of sufficient quality, and how do we know when and whether it is successful?

Before we begin another revolution, it might be worthwhile to pause and consider whether the school curriculum culture is resilient enough to consider permanent revolutions, where when one cycle is completed another is immediately begun. Although this can be a good idea, a curriculum needs time to 'bed in', so you might want to think about when to begin another revolution in the same area of study, bearing in mind that it doesn't have to be used to make wholesale changes and can pick up on minor problems should they occur.

It is necessary to develop a culture in which we look for incremental improvements as part of a continuous, ipsative process. The curriculum is never 'completed'. It is part of an ongoing conversation between leaders, teachers, pupils and other stakeholders, but it also needs to time to be 'enacted' by teachers and learned by the pupils.

Discussion

- How well has the curriculum culture been instilled?
- What could we do to improve this culture?
- Agree the next steps: which areas of our overall curriculum need to be reviewed?
- Do the short-, medium- and long-term milestones for reaching our curriculum goals require a process of more rapid or more gradual change?
- What lessons can we draw from the process, and what changes do we think need to be made to our approach and to our use of the curriculum wheel?

Each revolution can take things further, but remember to ensure changes are only made where necessary to improve the quality of the curriculum, make the teaching easier and make the learning more fulfilling.

A curriculum wheel is certainly not a new idea, but I hope you have found some of my tweaks to this basic idea to be interesting and/or useful. If so...

Onwards with the next revolution, comrades!

Acknowledgements

Heartfelt thanks are due to…

All at John Catt, especially Alex Sharratt for his patience and gentle nudging to get the project off the ground; Jonathan Barnes, for his enthusiasm and for seeing it through the early stages; and Isla McMillan, for her advice, insights and most excellent editing.

David Goodwin, for some revolutionary illustrations and his great graphical storytelling.

David Didau, for his helpful advice and input, especially in the 'assessment' section.

Tom Sherrington, for his advice and lovely foreword.

All involved with the Estonia curriculum project, especially Claire Stoneman for introducing me to the team. This project allowed me to float some ideas that had been percolating for some time. Thanks especially for the positive responses to the 'curriculum architecture/ shape' ideas and to Ed Vainker for his 'wheel'.

My family, for their love and support over the past few months.

And to you, for using this book.